T0128031

A Long Way from Ethiopia

A Journey Fueled by Fortitude, Optimism and Resilience

Zenebe Abebe

authorHOUSE®

AuthorHouse™
1663 Liberty Drive
Bloomington, IN 47403
www.authorhouse.com
Phone: 1 (800) 839-8640

Published by AuthorHouse   04/18/2018

ISBN: 978-1-5462-3671-9 (sc)
ISBN: 978-1-5462-3670-2 (e)

Library of Congress Control Number: 2018904249

Print information available on the last page.

Dedication

Dedicated to the following:

Ayelech Nadew—my mom, the most loving and pleasant person I have ever known.

Abebe Lekyalebet—my dad, a man with strong dedication to his family, a community organizer, a very funny person and a man of his word.

Mismake Abebe— my dear sister, she was the manager of all personal affairs within our family and the glue that held us together.

Acknowledgements

I would like to thank Katrina Pieri and Twila Albrecht who assisted me in editing my manuscript. They were very helpful in shaping and formatting the text before submitting it to my publisher.

I want to acknowledge my family; my wife Barbara, and my sons Kaleab and Ashenafi, who were very understanding and resilient during our nine moves from one state to another during their growing up years. We have done well together and this book is for you.

TIMELINE: EVENTS IN THE LIFE OF ZENEBE ABEBE

January 5, 1949	Zenebe Abebe born in Deder, Ethiopia
June 1971	Graduated from high school
August 12, 1972	Came to the U.S. for a college education
December 1974	Graduated from Hesston College
December 1975	Graduated from Goshen College
May 1978	Graduated with a Master's degree from Northern Illinois University
July 1978	Accepted a position at Goshen College
August 1979	Married Barbara in Memphis, TN
May 1981	First son born in Goshen, IN
July 1982	Co-led the Belize SST program with Barbara
December 1983	Zenebe's parents traveled from Ethiopia to the U.S. for a visit
August 1984	Enrolled in a Ph.D. program at Southern Illinois University
December 1984	Second son born in Illinois
May 1987	Graduated from Southern Illinois University

July 1987	Accepted the Asst. Dean of Students position at Manchester University
December 1989	Traveled to the former Soviet Union with thirty-seven students for a Cross Cultural Psychology study program
July 1990	First visit back to Ethiopia in 10 years
July 1991	Accepted the position of Director for the Multicultural Education program at Goshen College
April 1997	Awarded a Fulbright grant to Germany
June 1998	First trip to Ethiopia with Barbara and the kids
January 2002	Developed and led the first SST program to Ethiopia
July 2003	Accepted the Dean of Student Life Position at Fresno Pacific University in California
January 2008	Became the founding V.P. for Equity and Inclusion at Marion University in Wisconsin
June 2009	Moved to Indianapolis, IN
April 2011	Accepted the invitation to be the Executive Director for MCC Great Lakes

Table of Contents

Part I: Introduction

Preface

One day in early spring of 2010, I decided to go to my memory bank and retrieve what I could find of the fading memories of my past. I wanted to put on paper what is commonly known as a memoir.

A memoir is defined as, "a record of events by a person having intimate knowledge of their life account based on personal observation." In other words, it is an account of my personal life and experiences. In my case, it will be my autobiography or a published record of my journey. Writing it may have taken me several years, but I was determined to keep writing until I felt I was done telling part of my story.

I am convinced that personal stories enriched with unusual events in a person's life can be inspirational to others. For the most part, some personal stories can perhaps be new to most of the readers, especially if the experiences are shared from a cross-cultural perspective such as mine. I am not presenting facts, but a story. I am well aware that stories tell us more about a person than facts.

My story is most likely the same as that of every other Ethiopian growing up in the Harar Province. However, I know that my story is certainly different, as it should be, from those growing up in the United States.

As we all know, no two individual's stories are the same, and therefore, each person's story can be interesting to read. In my case, it is true that my siblings' journeys and mine started from the same point. They include similarities such as traveling on the same road, educational experiences being of the same background and orientation. While my journey in some ways, may have been similar to those of my brothers and sisters. To a certain degree, our stories may end up being totally unique to each of us, based on such factors as decision making, choice, judgment, and meanings that are imperative to us.

For example, I believe I am shaped by the following major factors in my life: I have lived on two continents, in three different countries and in five states. To that end, I will always be an Ethiopian and yet I am a part of the places and events that have shaped me.

My story is a mixture of many interesting events; some were of my own making and others occurred because of unexpected events beyond my control. As crazy as it may sound, this journey of mine started as unplanned and unsolicited. Most of all, the destination was often unknown to me, particularly in the beginning. Sometimes I was just moving, not knowing what the future would bring and having to trust in things beyond my control.

I believe that if any of our stories are told with courage and honesty, then there is potential for our stories to help us preserve family traditions. Perhaps they can serve the future generation as a point of reference of customs and cultures from those of us who are immigrants from the old world.

This is not a diary, nor is it intended to be a story of my success or accomplishments. Instead, it is a story of resilience, hope and determination. It is simply a summary record of my journey. It is best described as a story of relationships, joy, freedom and family.

For me, it is a story and reflection of responsibility, of good work ethics and service. It is a journey of faith, fellowship, challenges and affirmation from others. It is a journey of strong desire for knowledge. Perhaps it has become a journey of discovering the unknown.

Why Write?

I think writing this memoir has helped me say the following to my family: this is my story; what is yours? This is what I recorded on my journey. I am encouraging you to do the same with yours. I am passing on to my family what gave me the hope and motivation to get to where I am today.

I can say that I never had everything together like others think I did. I struggled, I failed, but I got up and started all over again. Sometimes it appeared to be a journey of trial and error, but it was always a journey of going forward, never back. My story can be summed up in the following words by Winston Churchill: "Success is walking from failure to failure with no loss of enthusiasm."

This reflection is about recognizing the journey itself not as the end, and it's about understanding that the end is when one has no access to the future. I believe that at the end of my journey, my story will begin, and I want to be the author of my story.

When I think about my reflection, I realize part of this interwoven and highly complex journey of mine may be subject to my siblings' judgment. I would also like to acknowledge my vulnerability and weakness, which contributed to my long, fascinating and successful journey.

In the process of documenting my journey, I spoke with my siblings and my children and learned that they were all excited for me and supportive of my writing. Perhaps now is a wonderful opportunity for me to say the following to them: I love you, thank you, grace to me and, I too, offer grace to you. One must understand that I come from a culture where public expression of emotion within the family is personal, and so expressions such as "I love you" are not practiced verbally and outwardly all the time. However, there's no question that we share all the emotions every human being experiences. To that end, we do love, feel, laugh, hurt, hope and cry.

In other words, through my writing, I will be able to say what needs to be said to members of my family. As stated above, I come from a culture where public expression of emotion is not very common, unlike in western culture. Because of that, I know that no one in my family will accuse me of having the attributes of being overly emotional and highly expressive. Instead, I know they will acknowledge that I am caring and loving. They will say that most of the time I took the lead when responding to the needs of family members.

To Say I Love You

Family is about love. I have been enriched by the love I received from family members, sometimes even when what I have done did not deserve the love given back. My family has been generous to me. It is hard for me to imagine where I could have ended up if I hadn't had their encouragement and support. My brothers and sisters looked at me as the one who could do nothing wrong, and in their eyes I always did right. For that I continue to love them.

To Say Thank You

Much of my gratitude goes to my family members. I have so much to thank them for, including their understanding, support and counsel as I was growing up and making decisions that were sometimes totally against the norm and the expectations of family traditions. I was given all the freedom and the permission to explore my potential in life. At least that was what I thought I understood.

Seeking Grace

As I was young, restless, older than most, and driven by ambition, I am sure my expectations drove some of my siblings crazy. I now recall there was a time when I felt I was always right, and to some extent was manipulative enough to marginalize any ideas that did not support mine. I expressed anger and disapproval of others' behavior many times; when I did not know what to do with anger back then, I nursed and dispensed it in the only way I knew how. As one of the older brothers, my voice carried weight and most of my brothers and sisters simply followed my lead.

I don't believe that any of my siblings nor my children have any resentments against me, but as I am not perfect, I am sure I have offended some of them and I thank them for their gift of graciousness and for believing in me.

On the other hand, I like to believe that maybe some of my siblings (the rebellious ones) may have benefited from the extra push, nagging, and occasional disapproval from me. It may have helped them get to where they are now. However, intentionally or not, I am sure I have stepped on some toes and I simply say opus, sorry for that.

To Offer Grace

It is inevitable that we will run into conflict, as it's in human nature. However, admitting fault is not easy for any of us. Managing conflict is a shared task and it can be resolved if only mistakes are admitted and grace is offered. As a young person without my current conflict resolution skills, I am sure I was disappointed by some, and perhaps I did not know what to do with this disappointment except to show my anger with the hope that the conflict would resolve itself. I am indeed ready to say you have my grace and that all is well. I believe we've all now reached a point where we can say sorry to one other, but with a promise to spell out future intentions so that the same thing doesn't happen again.

The Driving Force

Until recently the driving force for my behavior was fueled by unrecognized aptitude, which I will explain in a moment. As it has been said, there is a reaction for every action. It is important for my family to understand what my strengths are. That way they can understand the decisions I have made and the actions I have taken, or in other words, why I made certain decisions. How I behave, and how I respond to my environment can be explained by my personality, which I discovered later in my life. I took the Strengths Finder, which is also known as a psychological profile of personality. This is not unique to me; it is very universal. Every one of us has been created with some strength that is very unique to us. By now, I've done up to four different personality assessments, mostly out of curiosity. The one that stands out is the Strengths Finder. Strengths Finder always measures the presence of 34 talent themes.

I first took the Strengths Finder test (The Gallup Organization, Princeton, NJ) in 1996 and 2004, and then for the third time in 2008. The results of all three tests came back with the same strength themes.

By the way, everyone that takes the Strengths Finder will get a list of 34 themes that are ranked with the top 5 in the beginning of the list. Based on the Strengths Finder, also known as a psychological personality inventory, here are my top five "Signature Themes," all of which I affirm:

1. ACHIEVER ...

It was pointed out to me that I have a constant need for achievement. I feel that every day starts at zero, and by the end of the day I must achieve something tangible in order to feel good about myself. Additionally, if a day passes without some form of achievement, no matter how small, I feel dissatisfied. I am told and I affirm what was pointed out to me: I have the energy to work long hours without burning out. I am able to set the pace and define the level of productivity for my team.

2. FOCUS...

It was made clear to me that I need a focused "destination" for myself. This means that I frequently set goals to serve as my "compass," helping me to determine priorities and keep me on "course." I instinctively evaluate whether a particular action will help me move toward my goals.

3. ACTIVATOR ...

I learned that I am impatient for action. This is because I believe that only action can make things happen and lead to performance. In my view, action and thought is the same thing. Action is the best way to learn. So, once a decision is made, I must act.

4. COMMAND ...

It was pointed out to me that I am strong in the command strength, which really means that I have presence. I can take action and make decisions. It is true that because of this theme, I respond to conflict and help others take action quickly.

5. INPUT ...

Finally, emphasis was placed on how I have a craving to know more and to archive all kinds of information. It was suggested that I like to collect things for future references and cravings for knowledge, and I strongly agree with this.

This assessment should explain my behavior as guided by my strengths. I see it as a good gift and very much affirm and accept what I just recorded. This has been a good guide as I work with people. Since I did not invest in my strengths, I do not consider them as my private possessions, but I found them as crucial resources for explaining my behavior.

As I reflect on my journey, I want to pay attention to my experiences, which were perhaps guided by my strengths and shaped by my environment. This is about more than responding to where I came from and my corresponding social environment. As water takes the shape of its container, so I began adjusting to whatever environment I subjected myself to. I would like to focus on my upbringing, family, schooling, friends, siblings, education and choice of profession, faith, and resources, and on most of the events in my life that contributed to who I am today. It is not just about me but also the events, people, politics, history, and economics that impacted my journey.

The Past

Through the years, I became aware that only when I stop and think do I become excited and even more interested in my own past experiences. In turn, this fuels my interest to do well and to do better in whatever I am engaged in. There are times when I wonder if memories of the past control me, or if they are a source of strength to go forward.

For reasons I can't explain, my past, though it was at times tough and sometimes unpleasant, simply was what it was, no more or less than a human experience with all its challenges. So, I recall my past as being as pleasant as it possibly could have been. I have no regrets, only gratitude. That is why it makes me wonder how it all began, where I have been, and where I am now.

I can say with all honesty that life has been, and continues to be, an intriguing journey. It has been a life enriched with grace, love and compassion. I have nothing to say but to stay on course and continue the journey.

However, I noted that through it all, yes, I did face challenges, even if the good has outweighed the bad. Although I report about a lot of good experiences, I assure my readers that I did not leave out any major challenging events in my life.

I lived a life with an unpredictable future. There were many unknowns, including some unexpected and unimagined conflicts. To that end, the outcomes continued to be full of surprises and challenges, but I somehow always found a way out, or found resolution to my conflicts.

My Family

As I grow older and comparatively reflect on family and what it all means, my desire to tell my past becomes even stronger. However, relating my stories of growing up, sharing experiences, and helping others understand the impact of time, place and history, and where I come from, continues to be a challenge. Even my wife, Barbara, who visited Ethiopia three times and heard stories from my family, knows only a small fraction of my story.

I decided to write my story mainly for my family, perhaps because of my strong desire to share my life journey with my sons, nephews and nieces and, of course, my grandchildren Hannah and Noah Abebe, all of them born and raised in the United States.

I want my children to know about my birthplace, background, and roots, and about what I did growing up. I want them to know who my parents were and what they did for a living, how they raised us, what their values were, and what their expectations were for their children.

Sadly, going forward, none of my family in the United States will understand as much as I want them to, let alone fully relate to my experience. However, my hope is that maybe reading this story will give them some perspective as they deal with their own journeys.

I have taken my sons to my home country of Ethiopia, including to my birthplace of Deder and various historical sites. We visited museums together and I told them the history of the land from which I came. But, as time passed, I reached the conclusion that there are a lot of things even my sons, Kaleab and Ashenafi, do not know and would not fully understand about it. Where I grew up in Ethiopia is so different from where I raised my family in the U.S., mainly because of the complexity of culture, history, language and the general way of life. It's almost impossible to fully explain in such a way that people from another political, social and economic system can grasp the interpretation of my experience.

Sometimes I want to believe that Ashenafi, our youngest son who spent a semester in a study abroad program in the northern part of the country, may have some glimpse of what life is like for children growing up in Ethiopia. His experience with school children in the area where he did his service assignment may have given him some idea of how growing up in Ethiopia could be different than in the U.S.

Stories he heard from his newly acquainted relatives about my upbringing may have opened his eyes and probed his mind, and may have given him more life issues to ponder for years to come. However, I am afraid it was not enough for him to recognize the whole story.

My immediate family in America can only understand what they saw and where I am now. They can't understand as much about where I came from. In other words, I'd like them to understand the past, but they only understand what they see at the present. The outcome of my journey was partially dictated by time, place and events that I was part of, as well as by my personal experiences. I believe the impacts of events in my life provide the background to help define my life and family. This is in addition to the impacts of environment and politics that also contributed to shaping my entire life. I know that my family clearly understands that I came to the States for an education.

My coming to the States for education was one thing, and it was a personal decision, but staying here for the rest of my life was perhaps another thing and could be labeled as unplanned, which came about because of politics.

As I'll explain later, in 1972, I left Ethiopia to come to the United States on a student visa for college education. Two years later, in 1974, a Marxist revolution took place in the country, which made it impossible for me to go back after college.

Moving Forward

Where I am now in life has more meaning for me only when I look back and remember my past experiences. Looking back, my experience always made feel good about my past, fulfilled, and at peace. The future looks promising. For the most part, as strange as it may seem, I am content and I have less desire for more things in my life. Although I am grateful for where I am in life, the past was by no means without challenges and struggles.

Like so many others around me, growing up, I had the privilege of experiencing the joy of hugging and rejoicing great things that happened to me, and at the same time shouldering all the unpleasant challenges in life. However, I can't say for sure that I had more problems than others, nor can I say that God burdened me with more than I could handle.

However difficult the challenge may have been at the time, I always saw the future as bright and hopeful. For some reasons that I cannot explain, no matter what the challenges were, I always saw the potential for new possibilities for change around me.

For me, the path I had taken from where I was to where I am now, continues to be fascinating. Perhaps the drive in me can't be explained except by simply saying that it was fueled by unexplainable activities in my brain, and by the blood that flows from my heart to sustain me and give me hope and inspiration.

No matter how hopeful or discouraging my journey may have been at times, the mix of experiences in life always served me as a foundation for the new chapter yet to come. At this point in my life, it is becoming clear to me that the past gives me joy. Remembering how things were in my childhood brings me unexplainable joy. I am well aware that I just can't live in the past, but it surely feels good to at least think about it. I love talking about my days growing up. I particularly love talking about my family.

So, I will start telling my story from the beginning. Let me take you on a journey to this ancient land of mine (Ethiopia) where my journey began.

Part II: Growing Up in Ethiopia

My Siblings

Before I begin describing my experience growing up in Ethiopia, I will tell you a little about my siblings.

Of my parents' eight children, six of us are boys and two are girls. I have two older siblings: an older brother and an older sister. The gap between the six younger siblings averages about two years. Our older sister is much older than our older brother, with the gap closer to ten years. While growing up, we were very close and did a lot of things together.

Since there was no high school in our town at the age when we were ready to go to high school, the older and younger siblings especially started to grow apart. Going to college made this situation even worse, because the four boys came to the United States and the other four stayed at home for various reasons. In the 70's and 80's, because of the political situation in Ethiopia, those of us here in the States were unable to travel and see our parents for over ten years.

Looking back, I can't even imagine how our parents felt when they were not able to see us for this long period of time. Missing us must have been a horrible experience for them.

To return to the subject of my siblings, I am going to give each of them an Amharic nickname, translated to English, as I write about each of them. The comments below are simply my observations, so some may not totally agree with my comments. I invited some of my brothers to read my comments about each of my siblings and to give me feedback. I am grateful to them for their candid feedback. More than anything else, this is intended to be humorous and is in no way meant to be malicious. I do understand that they all know I care about each of them, and that I love them all.

Tadelech, also known as Ababa (Shererit):

She is one of the most hardworking persons I have ever known. She is a strong person with a strong will, and she is always in command. She works like a spider, and whatever she does, she does well. She is the oldest child and always has high energy. She's an independent and proud lady. Additionally, she survived many tragedies, including the loss of two of her daughters who were both in their 40's. As a single mother she raised three children, and she also raised five grandchildren after Kelemua was murdered. Also, she was responsible for raising Asegedech's children.

Ababa was able to support herself and also her three children and five grandchildren. Even when she did not have enough and was struggling to make ends meet, she never asked for help. The only words she knows how to say are "thank you." She has one son whom she's very proud of and admires. It is very interesting that Tadelech, who was the most dependent on her son and the rest of us, has now become the person to go to. When we travel to Ethiopia, we stay at Tadelech's home, and she is more than happy to host us.

Gedamu (Ato Desalgne):

One wonders what makes my older brother Gedamu laugh. He is always joyful and happy. He was a smart student in Grammar School and it appears that he was always a follower. He has eight children just like our parents. I always wonder if Gedamu had any big plans or ambitions as an adolescent or young adult. He decided not to go to high school or college. He graduated from the police academy and retired early. It was always my wish for Gedamu to aim high. Now, I always wonder what would have happened if Gedamu had continued his education through college.

Teshome (Ato Atenkugn):

Growing up, Teshome did his own things. For the most part, he was an observer and was not involved in too many peer conflicts, and did not get in trouble. He did not seem to be bothered by what was going on around him. He shuns conflicts and rarely offers nonacademic advice to others. As a child, he slept like there was no tomorrow, and when it came to school, he was at the top of his class and always did well. He was self-motivated and always gave the impression that he knew what he wanted. He likes to dress up, a habit he picked up from my father and also from his experience in high school.

Solomon (Ato Chernet):

Among our family members, Solomon is known for his generosity and kindness. He, too, did well academically. He's a person who is devoted to pleasing everyone with whom he comes into contact. It seems that a lot of people always did, and still continue to, take advantage of Solomon's generosity. Knowingly or otherwise, Solomon never seemed to mind what was going on. He doesn't get involved in other people's affairs, though he's always kind to them. He still continues to be the most giving and caring brother I have known.

Kelemua Abebe (Weyzero Gedyelesh):

Kelemua was our niece, a daughter of my older sister, who was raised by my parents from day one. She was beautiful and always wore a striking smile. She had straight, long and dark silky hair over her shoulders. She always struggled academically and perhaps wasn't sure about what she wanted to do in life. She was married three times and was a single mother who raised three children alone. Kelemua's life ended in tragedy during an uprising in our town: she was murdered in 1991 by political operatives and extremists of the Oromo movement, when the Ethiopian People's Revolutionary Democratic Front (EPRDF) was consolidating power. I wonder what would have happened if Kelemua had shown an interest in finishing high school and even college.

Mismake (Agafari or Astedadari Manager):

Like Kelemua, Mismake is no longer with us. She died on April 4, 2011, in Indianapolis. Further on in this memoir you will read some short comments I wrote about her. I still can't figure out how she held our family together. She managed both family and non-family members' affairs. She managed the good, the bad, the crazy, the sick, the drunk, the educated and the uneducated, the law abiders and the criminals, the family and also the outsiders. When she died all hell broke loose. Our family has never been the same since her death. I sometimes wonder if Mismake had the same opportunity that I and all her brothers had, like going to college, how her life may have been different.

Sisay (Ato Indashow):

Sisay, like Solomon, would give his life for his family. By some sheer bad luck he became a nomad. Because of his involvement in politics in Ethiopia, he had to flee the country. He lived in different countries as a refugee and was separated from his family for years. Now, he lives in Amsterdam with his family.

As a child, Sisay simply was uninterested to go to school and dropped out when he was in sixth grade. None of us could convince him that he could benefit from education, and that he needed to stay in school. He lived in three different countries, not by choice, but because he had to flee. He has mastered at least four different languages and is very adaptive. He never gives up. I wish Sisay had had the opportunity to study in some vocational center where he may have developed his gifts. As the saying goes, "Gobzena chis Mewcha ayatam." This means that a daring person and smoke will always find a way to escape.

Tamene (Ato Baytewar):

Because Tamene was the baby (the last child) in our family, and because of the Marxist revolution, he may have developed a different set of values for himself. Sometimes, he is hard to read, and it's difficult to understand what he's thinking, if he's even thinking about anything at all. I am not sure if he has any philosophical stance about life, family or community. I have no idea how he has been affected by the Marxist ideology, or by simply being away from home as a young adult.

There seems to be a big gap and disconnect between most of his siblings and him, probably due to the fact that we'd already left home when he was still in primary school. His life also became more complicated when his own family became a challenge to him. He did well in college and he was able to secure a profession as good as those of the rest of us. However, at least to me, it appeared that something was missing for him and none of us were able to figure it out. His relationships with his siblings appear to be irregular and somewhat superficial. Particularly, after our sister Mismake's death, he became even more distanced and unreachable. Maybe this will all pass one day.

Parenting for Life

If I take the liberty to speak on behalf of my siblings, we are who we are today because of our parents' outlook in life and the impact of their relationship with each of us in their parenting style. Our parents surrounded us with care, love and resources to help us carry the day. There was no long-term planning for education, health care, career or retirement. They lived in the present, not worrying about the next day and leaving tomorrow totally to God.

Our parents were good at teaching us life skills. It was clear to them, in their own context, that what was important was to serve and be good to others. It was important to them that we not only learn how to survive, but to leave behind a good name or legacy. For our parents, it was important to serve others whenever possible. It is no wonder that our behaviors are so much like those of our parents. I can say that our parents did not teach their children what to do in life, but instead expected their children to watch and learn from them. We are much like our parents when it comes to the values we continue to have for family and work.

Growing up, we respected our elders as we were told to do. We lived as a community that cared for each other, and we came from a strong Christian tradition. Most of all, we were taught to determine our own destiny. When we came to the United States, we left all that good tradition behind us in Ethiopia for what we imagined to be possible.

Of course, our plan initially was to simply get bachelor's degrees and then return home, with the hope of landing good jobs that the country had to offer at that time. Yet, once we got here, despite the opportunities and the potential for possibilities to learn and grow, we also encountered the misunderstandings and confusion to be expected in a new culture.

First, the new culture made me even more determined to enjoy memories of my past. I have an ongoing wish to see and visit the places where I grew up, but more and more this is becoming an impossible reality because of where I am in my life now. I long for my childhood friends, the playgrounds, the farm life, the school I attended and the kind of work I performed growing up.

Second, for me, I find that my entire "growing up" experience is worth recalling and talking about. I am finding it hard to speak about my past without including my parents in the narrative. Third, for me, my past has become the energy that fuels my future.

Since I am physically removed from where I grew up, and since I can't be there, I will continue to talk about it now, because that is what gave me a foundation on which to build.

Values to Hold and Cherish

In the town of Deder, where I grew up, the family structure was different. The culture and the way of life where I am now are completely different from the one I left behind.

It was, and still is, a place where a major part of the culture involves giving respect to parents and older people. Parental expectations of children, and children's expectations of their parents, are different and mutually respectful.

Information sharing and modes of communication were totally different; they were simple and good.

It was a place, or a culture, where relationships are not defined by wealth or by material possessions, but by love of family and quality of time spent in supporting one another or caring for one another, which in turn changes the family dynamics.

At a very young age, I picked up one important value from my parents: interest in others. I developed a strong interest in the affairs of my brothers, sisters, parents and other relatives. I had one simple goal: to be a catalyst to help them carry on their passion, perhaps in what they wanted to become. Even then, somehow, I was able to see the potential in every one of my brothers and sisters to achieve their desires. I decided to join them in making their dreams come true.

I had the sense that all the positive energy, hard work, good ethics and the desire to succeed that our parents impressed on us would not be in vain.

Growing up, we observed our parents not only work hard, but work at many different jobs in order to provide for their children. Our parents believed in hard work and they were not ashamed of it. They taught us that dignity and honor come with work, and that work is what people do to support family and to get ahead.

I always believed then, and still do, that someday, somewhere, and somehow, we are destined to be good citizens, making differences in any community we decide to live.

Others in My Journey

I believe that any measureable and meaningful human experience does not take place in a vacuum. I also want to point out that my journey did not take place without the impact of others in my life. However, early on I learned that it is my decision to determine the boundaries, involvement and quality of friends in my life. I was blessed with family and the friendship of others, in addition to guidance and mentorship, which were available to me if and when I needed them.

My experience is only part of the larger experience around me. I was nurtured especially by family members, elders, community leaders, teachers and peers.

Back then, I was, and even now I am, comfortable with helping anyone in need. At the same time, I was open to asking for help if I was in need.

I learned early on from my parents to respect people for who they are, not for what they do or have. I learned that I will do whatever it takes to make an honest living by working hard. I learned that only by respecting myself can I respect others.

I came to believe that we (humans) impact one another through our day-to-day interactions, and that without these interactions our existence would be less meaningful. I also learned to stand up for what I believe in.

I gave myself permission to defend my values and to not allow anyone to push their values on me. I do respect authority, but I do not understand nor respect unearned or undeserved power over me.

I discovered that helping others is the most joy-producing act of kindness I can ever experience. I learned early on from my parents that sharing what I have, helping others when I can, and mentoring and empowering others must be part of what makes me human.

This is the most precious value any parent can pass on to their children and I was fortunate to have had the privilege to inherit this gift from my parents.

So, this was my beginning that led me to become who I am today. I believe the beginning provided a good push for a long journey that continues to this day.

My Parents

As I mentioned above, my mom and dad were the parents of eight children. I have five brothers and we each have two sisters. I am the third child in the family, with an older sister and an older brother. Others in my family may have heard different stories, but I was told that I was the first to be born in the Harar Province after my parents migrated from the northern part of Ethiopia (Minjar), soon after the Italian war. My older sister, Tadelech, and my older brother, Gedamu, were born in the northern part of Ethiopia. The rest of our extended family members lived in about a fifty to seventy mile radius around the town of Deder.

My mother was very soft spoken, kind, and loving. She always wore a striking smile and was very respected by our neighbors, who always admired each child for their individual ability and didn't compare one child to another. My mother not only cared for us, but was also the organizer and total manager of our affairs. She worked side by side with my dad to raise eight children and encouraged us to go to school.

My mother's background and her experience growing up were very different from my father's. We did not know much about her childhood days. She seldom talked about it. We were told that my mother's parents both died when she was still an infant. As the story was told to us, she lost her parents to an epidemic known by locals as the November outbreak or disease (also known as Yehedar beshita in Amharic). It killed thousands of people in the Harar Province. She was raised by her aunt, Zewditu, who we got to know as we were growing up. Aunt Zewditu was very caring and generous, and very protective whenever she came to our home to visit, or when we went to see her in her home in Kulube (a well-known town in Ethiopia).

My mother always said to us "never leave your house with an empty stomach," meaning, always eat your breakfast before you leave the house, for you do not know what you are going to face during the day.

My father was a person with unshakable confidence. He was self-assured and always said to his children, "don't say 'I don't know' or 'I can't.'" He believed that one should always attempt to fix what is not working, or to try one's best before saying "I can't" or "I don't know," or asking for help. He always had high expectations for both himself and his children. He was a well-mannered, well-spoken, community member. He was also a well-dressed and happy man, a respected leader, and a man with presence, style and confidence.

Among other things, I remember one interesting quality about my father; he made things happen. He was good at convincing people to join him in community projects. Although he was an uneducated man, he was blessed and enriched with wit and wisdom. He was a funny man who made everyone around him laugh. I can simply describe my family as hard-working, loving, nurturing, and strong-willed. We were engaged members of our community.

Both of my parents spoke two languages fluently (as did most community members). My father additionally spoke Italian, which might have contributed to our desire to learn more than one language.

Where We Lived

My home town, Deder, was a breath-taking, picturesque place surrounded by magnificent mountains. Now, an estimated 252,524 people live in the region. The altitude of this region ranges from 1,200-3,140 meters above sea level. We lived at the foot of a mountain to the west that rose about three miles up at about 80 degrees. About two miles east of the house where I grew up, the land drops down about another three miles into a valley. All kinds of tropical fruits and coffee are grown there. To the north and south of my home, the range of mountains stretches as far as one can see. Near my home, no matter in which direction you focus your gaze, it looks like the mountain is about to touch the sky. This is a mountain covered with trees and shrubs, providing the community with building materials and firewood. The mountain is also home to many wild animals, such as deer, porcupines, wild pigs and more. Growing up, it was not unusual for me and my friends to be climbing this mountain for one reason or another.

We lived near the town of Deder, where farming was the heart and soul of the community. All of our neighbors had children, so we had friends to play with all the time. We lived by the main road that went to the town of Deder, where people walked to go shopping, including selling and buying. It was not unusual for my mom or dad to walk to the street by our home and buy whatever they needed from people going to the market. They did this simply by asking them to stop and then negotiating prices. For example, my parents could buy such things from the roadside as milk (if we were not producing our own), coffee, grains, spices, firewood, chickens, goats, etc. The list goes on.

At one point, we had three small to medium sized houses in the same compound. In the "big house," as we called it, we all got together in the evenings. No matter what, it was a home where we all looked forward to gathering at the end of the day. We ate together, we worked together, and we all lived together in the same home for all those years when I was growing up. Every evening, we enjoyed listening to our father play the kirar (a six-string traditional Ethiopian instrument) for us. I remember watching the process and the time it took my father to build his own instrument. It was a complex and long process, but he wanted us to see the process with the hope that one of his children would pick up the interest of playing the kirar. I don't think it happened, ironically we all have the instrument in our homes. I believe Tamenen built one when he was in college as his arts class project.

I always thought we had just enough. My mother wanted to be sure that we always had enough to eat. Even when food became scarce at times, we never starved. In fact, our parents always wanted us to believe we had plenty.

My mother, even though she was very quiet, she was the manager of our affairs. She planned our daily menu and always had snacks when we came home from school. Her main concern was how we behaved at school. She wanted us to be known for good character at school and in our neighborhood. My mother wanted to be sure that we kept our family name in good standing. Perhaps, for my parents keeping track of eight children, and each child's affairs may have been a challenge for them, but I never heard them complaining.

When I think about it, even to this day, I wonder how my parents were able to raise eight children. When I think back, I still wonder how on earth my parents continued to be at ease and happy with such a responsibility.

Faith

My parents belonged to the Ethiopian Coptic Church, as all Amhara groups in Ethiopia did. They were very religious and serious about observing all of the religious holidays. All of us very much looked forward to these holidays because of the special foods and events that came with them.

My faith journey was also special, and in many ways unique compared to my siblings. Since I was born into an Ethiopian Orthodox family, I was baptized at 40 days after birth. That made me a Christian and a member of the Orthodox Church by birth. My faith influence came from my parents' devoted faith within the Orthodox Church.

I was sent to preschool at a religious prep school and went on to study Geez (the church language). Eventually, I was inducted into an Arclight boy's duty at the church. This lasted until I discovered the Mennonite grade school, where I was introduced to a Protestant religion, which actually affirmed my faith. Both the Orthodox followers and Protestants believe in the trinity. The main difference, among other things, is that the Biblical teaching emphasis for the Orthodox Church is on the Old Testament, while the Biblical teaching emphasis for Protestants is on the New Testament. Of course, when it came to worship and rituals, they were far apart and had no similarities.

My Parents' Profession

My parents were farmers and I have the most pleasant memory of that part of my growing up experience. Almost all of the adults in our community were known as farmers, which was the only profession available for them and the only way to support a family. I would estimate the percentage of farmers to be about 90 percent of the population of that region. These farmers used pre-19th century tools. This means that a farmer could not farm without oxen, which were used to plow the land. Here, I am talking about subsistence farmers who mainly farmed to meet the needs of their families. Life was simple and yet hard for most people.

I would think that given the lack of education and adequate medical care, life expectancy may not have been more than 50 years at that time. Amazingly, my mother died at age 75 from pneumonia and my father died at age 98 from old age. My father's older sister died at age 105, and another sister died at age 95. It would appear that there are some strong genes that want to stay around, and that we should be prepared to live longer.

My parents were respected members of the community. They were farmers who did not have their own land to farm. They were tenant, or subsistence, farmers like every other family in our region. The only land they owned was the plot that our house was built on, with a backyard for a garden. However, my parents owned all kinds of farm animals: cows, oxen, donkeys, goats, sheep and chickens.

I was told that, when I was born, my parents had over 30 cows, in addition to other livestock, and that they were considered well-to-do in their community at that time.

My older sister, Tadelech, told me that on the day of my baptism, my parents wanted to express their joy by butchering a cow that would feed the entire community. In those days, only the well-to-do could afford to show off how rich they were by way of planned parties.

One of the things our father did on the side, when he was not farming, was serving the community as a butcher. My father would buy a cow and butcher it as a business to make money. The community would buy the meat. Normally we'd make some money and most of the time there would be enough meat for the family to last for a week or two. Because of that, our family always enjoyed fresh meat, and since we were farmers, there was always milk to drink and even some to sell for cash.

As I recall, my parents would contract land to farm from two to three different landowners each year. They may have changed landowners from year to year, but they stayed with this one particular landowner for many years. I believe all of my brothers and sisters would remember a landowner called Wyzero Alemitu. I remember when we farmed Alemitu's land in three different locations. The size of the land we farmed at each location did not exceed 15 acres.

Most of the land we farmed was between one to three miles away from our home. This is significant because, as I'll explain in more detail later, every day, in the morning before school and in the evening after school, that is where my brothers and I went to help with the farm work.

Contractual Agreements for Tenant Farmers

In almost all cases in the farming land contractual agreements, the farmer agreed to fertilize, take care of the land, and farm it for whatever grain that particular parcel of land was suited for. The landowner would receive one-third of what the land produced, and the other two-thirds would go to the farmer.

This sounds very simple, however, because farm work was so labor-intensive at the time of harvest, most farmers felt robbed. The farmer also had no guarantee to continue to farm the same land. In other words, the contract meant the farmer was at the mercy of the landowner. The following year, the landowner normally has the option to switch the contract to another tenet if he or she wished.

There is a memory that's never left me of one particular year, during harvest time, when I was around 12 or 13 years old. I remember how I was so disappointed to see that one-third of the grain we'd worked hard to grow, and had harvested that season, was going to the landowner. It may have been a fair deal for all the parties involved, but economically it was not clear to me if this arrangement would benefit the landowner more than the tenants. How I wished I had enough money so I could purchase farmland for my parents.

Regardless of the yield, the landowner got their one-third of the share. On the other hand, the tenant, who may have had many mouths to feed, had no other options. Looking back now, I can simply say that it was nothing but an economic entrapment for the tenants. There was nothing they could do about it.

I used to think that if it were our land, we wouldn't have to give away what we worked for. For me, this was an issue associated with fairness. If my parents were to pay cash for the land, instead of giving part of the grain to the landowner, they may not have been able to afford it because this was the only cash crop they had.

For farmers, the only source of cash came from the sale of the grain they harvested. Some of the tenants had to sell their animals to pay debts and other family-related bills. However, what is amazing is that through everything involved in this seemingly unfair system, people were happy and didn't complain too much, unless it happened to be a bad year for farmers.

This unfair system was so entrenched on both sides of the society (the haves and the have not's) that no one wanted to do anything about it until 1974, when the Marxist revolution (as I'll explain further on) turned it upside down. At this point, land ownership totally went to the central government.

The Meaning of Work

I owe a great debt to my parents for teaching me that the concepts of "a job" and "work" have a meaning. This meaning involves independence. Furthermore, whatever we do for a living, our parents emphasized that our work must have some purpose to life.

Our family believed in a good work ethic. This reminds me of a phrase I once heard from a college student: "work is work." I learned this phrase from an international student who valued work no matter what. The student worked for my wife, and when Barbara asked the student which kind of work she preferred, the student who valued work simply said, "work is work."

"Work is work," was also my father's philosophy. Off season, when my father was not busy with farm work, he was either doing some carpentry work, buying and selling things, fishing to sell, trading coffee, or doing whatever else was available to him and could earn him a profit. This provided him with extra income to pay for our clothing and other necessary items to support the family. I believe my parents' attitude about the kind of work they did, in order to make a living and support a family, contributed to the strong work ethic that developed among my brothers and sisters. This work ethic has sustained us to this day.

My mother, on the other hand, was always busy keeping all of us happy and fed. She washed our clothes and did all of the motherly things that needed to be done. My mother was easygoing, unassuming, gentle and always hopeful. She was the peace-maker not only at home but in our small community.

Also, my mother tried to make money by making homemade drinks to sell. Everyone in our community made homemade beer (tella), which is made out of barley. One container (a barrel) would hold about 10 gallons of the drink. If my mother sold a good portion of the container, she would be able to make some cash to supplement my fathers' and her income, which as mentioned above, came from the income of selling grain or the extra income from my father's part-time work.

My parents held onto any job they could, whether they liked it or not. Of course, there wasn't much to choose from, but they did what they had to do in order to support the family. As all children do, we took our parents for granted. I am not sure if I said to them how much I appreciated their efforts, their hard work and, most of all, the sacrifices they made in order to make our lives better than theirs. I know it is too late now, but I still thank them and remember them for their commitment and persistence.

Growing Up in Deder

This is the memory that will never leave me: What I remember about my past is that my family was always happy and loving. Most of all, my brothers and sisters got along. However, the story I am about to share with you may sound unreal and out of the ordinary to some of you. Believe me, it is often that way for me too, however, because of time, place, and culture, that was the way it was.

On the other hand, no matter how it sounds, that was then and that was the experience and it was part of the journey. The experience I am about to share with you made me who I am today. Since I did not know any different, or have any other option, I always thought how we were raised was the norm, and that everyone was in the same situation.

All parents from my area had a minimum expectation for their children: work on the farm. My parents' expectations were no different from those of other parents. I must have been about 6 or 7 years old, and every morning I remember getting up at 5 or 6 AM to help my father at the farm. After the work at the farm was done, I would come back to eat breakfast and then leave, just in time to make it to school. That was also the time to complete homework, if possible. Because our parents never went to school, they had no understanding of homework, let alone what it takes to get ready for an exam.

During the evening, soon after school was out, we would go home, get some snacks and then head off to a particular farm. We would help with the farm animals and whatever else our father wanted us to help him with. We worked until it was dark. This went on, day in and day out, year after year, in winter and summer. Where I grew up, this kind of expectation for children was not out of the ordinary.

When it came to school work, we were on our own. It was almost a sink or swim situation. If you made it, fine, and if not, there was always work on the farm. In other words, if a child couldn't make it, it was totally the fault of the child and not the teacher or parents. I recall now that our parents' main concern was that we behaved well at school. At the end of the semester, my parents' main interest was in the grade we earned for our behavior, known as tebay or geregebent. In English it means "character." In other words, a letter grade—A, B, or C—was assigned for our behavior every semester.

If we did not score high on good behavior, we knew we were in trouble. More than anything, our parents wanted us to become respected citizens and contributing members of society. My parents always believed and communicated to us that good character would serve us well in life.

As I mentioned earlier under the "Faith" section, I started my primary education in the Orthodox Church school system. This is where I learned to read and write in Fedel (the Ethiopian alphabet, all 270 letters (or characters) of it) and Geez numbers. This is where I learned to memorize prayer, and other church chanting's, in the ancient Ethiopian language of Geez. Geez to Amharic is like Latin is to English in a Catholic Church. The one problem with Geez numbers is that they are cumbersome. There is also no "zero," so it cannot be used to add or subtract.

As soon as I discovered that, and after I realized that some of my friends were able to add and subtract in Roman numbers, and had started speaking beginner's English, I decided to go to a private (Mission) school, which actually cost money to attend. Since my parents were not able to pay the school fees for all of their children, I decided to pay for tuition by working after school and on weekends. I believe Gedamu, Teshome and Solomon did the same thing.

Mildred Histand, a missionary school teacher from Ephrata, PA, introduced me to the idea of self-help by giving me an after-school job to pay for school. This began in first grade. Mildred was not only a teacher but also a social worker and a good friend. As a child, my first paid job involved cleaning after school and on weekends. Additionally, I was given a job Saturdays that allowed me to bring in extra income. What was interesting about that job is that, to this day, I do not know what my pay was per hour or per week. Back then, I did not care to know; my only concerns were that the school fees were paid and I was happy. Mildred and I stayed in touch through my college days, and we even lived in the same community (Goshen, IN) until she passed away. She was my best teacher and mentor, and she was a good friend.

This was also a time and place where children grew up without the availability of manufactured toys or sports stores. There may have been some available on a smaller scale, but it was not affordable for most of the kids in my community. Such an idea was foreign to begin with, and it was not a priority in agrarian society. We simply created our own toys. We built cars out of mud, wood or scrap metals.

What it Meant to Go to School

Schooling for children was not a right but a privilege. For the most part, it was up to the parents to decide whether a child would go to school. If parents wanted to keep a child home and have them be, say, a goat herder or a helper on the farm, that was up to them.

There was no intervention by the government. Growing up in Deder, I could tell that children were seen as an asset, so farm work assumed a higher priority than education.

For our parents, measuring the outcome of farming was a lot easier than trying to imagine the benefit that would come years down the line if their children went to school. There were no benchmarks to help them see the benefit of education. At that time, since there weren't too many people educated beyond eighth grade, it was hard for parents to measure the outcomes of receiving an education.

I have no doubt that many of my friends who grew up with me in this ancient land have their own stories to tell. Some of our stories may have common threads that could blow the minds of those who live in this relatively new land we call the USA.

The fact is that most of us grew up in towns with school systems that had no library books, no parent's counsel, and in some places, no good playground for students. Since there were no textbooks, if we wanted to learn, it was up to us to write down everything the teacher said in class, and to copy down everything from the chalkboard.

Since my parents can't pay tuition for me and my brothers, I decided I pay for school from first grade through sixth grade. I give some credit to my former grade school teacher, Mildred Histand, whom I introduced earlier. Some of the money I earned from work (that I mentioned earlier) came from cleaning the classroom after school, working in my teacher's garden, and splitting firewood over the weekends.

For most of us, we may have gained the motivation and aspiration to go to school simply by observing that our parents couldn't read or write. Even though Ethiopia has had its own alphabet for thousands of years, schooling was always left to the aristocrats, nobles and clergies, not to the wider public.

As each of us began our journey, we encountered many events along the way. Mine is no different in that sense, but perhaps it is unique and interesting in its own way. We became more creative and applied the following saying to our lives: "Creativity is the mother of invention."

Unique or not, our personal journeys, for the most part, can tell our human experiences as they should. Our human experiences are not always packaged, nice and simple. For most people, personal stories will include sad events, happy moments and perhaps stories that are life-changing regardless of their impact.

The beginning of the summer just before I started seventh grade, I decided to drop out of school to begin a two-year training at a local hospital.

Dresser School (Health Assistance Training)

The main purpose of the health assistance training program was for the country to make health care available, mainly in rural areas. In a country where health care providers were limited, the government encouraged missionaries to develop health training centers across the country. The training center where I was trained was one of several in the country.

The program was called "Dresser School" or "Health Assistance Training." My main objective was to work and earn money so I could support my parents. For anyone to obtain a well-paying job, one needed the required skills that would help one move up another level on the salary scale. So, I decided to join the first health care training the Deder hospital ever launched. I was one of five in its first cohort. We knew that when one completes this type of training, there is always an opportunity to work in the health care system.

As I stated earlier, my main purpose for dropping out of school and joining this training was in part to support my parents. When I look back, I realize my decision was also strategic, because it was also meant to help my brothers and sisters continue their education so they could become self-sufficient. I really did not want any of my siblings to drop out of school like I did because of finances. I saw my parents struggling to support eight children. I also noticed that the income from the farm was not enough to support our family. Our family home was too old for another renovation. I decided to do something about it and, of course, the only way to do that was to get into this special health care training program.

The two-year health training was like a watered-down version of the curriculum offered in nursing schools. It may have been a scaled down version of a full scale traditional nursing curriculum, but all the nursing curriculum topics were fairly well covered, and it was an intensive two-year training program.

When I look back, it amazes me that we were able to follow along with this training in a foreign language. To begin with, the English language is a difficult one to learn. On top of that we had to deal with medical terminologies, which are hard to understand. Most of these words had Latin or German roots, which made it even more difficult for Ethiopians to pronounce.

For the sake of my readers (my American family), I will use terms they can easily understand when describing the following health training experience. But most of you, if not all, will have a hard time understanding that I am actually a health professional, at least at the level of a registered nurse.

To help me explain what the training was like, and what the purpose of the training was, I asked two of my trainers, Dr. Jose Burkholder, a missionary medical doctor from Canada, to write a paragraph or two. He put it this way:

> *"Deder Dresser School,' as it was called, was begun specifically so we would have trained people to do the work. Nazareth Health Care School, which came later, also included this practical training as well as with the goal to give extensive teaching. The courses included some anatomy and physiology, common diseases and treatment, and some pharmacology as well as how to care for patients. Patient care included: all vital signs such as Temperature, Pulse, Respiration, Blood Pressure, how to give injections, IM, IV, and Subcutaneous. Your Learning Lab, X-ray and Operating Room as you scrubbed to assist doctors in major surgeries all involved on the spot training as you went along. Eventually, trainees were able to diagnose and treat patients with supervision from missionary nurses and doctors."*

My mentor, Dr. Paul T. Yoder, actually started the Deder training school. He wrote the following observation:

"The Nazareth Health Training School was begun to train Ethiopians the rudimentary elements in providing patient care in the Haile Mariam Mamo Memorial Hospital, in Nazareth, Ethiopia. Initially, it began with 'elementary health education.' Students who completed this one-year training were qualified to provide better care to patients in the hospital. Later, the 'Advanced health care course' was added for selected students from the elementary year for further training, including diagnostic skills and improved knowledge of prescribing appropriate therapy for patients.

"The Nazareth Health Training School was begun to train Ethiopians the rudimentary elements in providing patient care in the Haile Mariam Mamo Memorial Hospital, in Nazareth, Ethiopia. Initially, it began with 'elementary health education.' Students who completed this one-year training were qualified to provide better care to patients in the hospital. Later, the 'Advanced health care course' was added for selected students from the elementary year for further training, including diagnostic skills and improved knowledge of prescribing appropriate therapy for patients.

"The intent was to have trained personnel to provide care for hospitalized patients. As more health care students received advanced training they became aware that by establishing clinics in remote areas of Ethiopia, they could care for many patients. Furthermore, the income they received by operating a clinic provided for better income. Halamariem Mamo Memorial Hospital (HMMMH) personnel saw this as an avenue to provide better health care throughout Ethiopia.

> *"This training provided more and more qualified health care providers to operate clinics throughout Ethiopia, particularly where health care resources were strictly limited. The demand*

I also invited two of my friends who went through the same training to write a bit about what the health training meant to them. Here are the responses from one friend to some questions I asked him about his time as a health care trainee in Ethiopia:

> *"When I had no opportunity for further education in my home area of Dembi Dolo. I heard about the Dresser Bible School (Health Care Training). This news gave me hope and a future. It led me to my lifelong profession in Pharmacy.*
>
> *"The health care training was a gate opener for high school and allowed me to work in the evenings while going to high school during the day.*
>
> *"Health care training instilled in me an early desire to pursue medicine and eventually helped me to decide on the field of Pharmacy.*
>
> *"I was in charge of the hospital during the evening shift at the HMMMH Hospital. This taught me to supervise as well as provide service to the ill and the injured. It's great to be able to save lives.*

> "Health care training prepared me for what I came to the U.S. for, which was to pursue Pharmacy. Educational opportunities were limited in Ethiopia so the standard time to start health care training was after elementary school.
>
> "I explained my health care training to people in the U.S. by comparing it to a Licensed Practical Nurse and sometimes even to a Registered Nurse."

During my interview with my second friend, he said the following:

> "I served in the area as the only health provider. I was a part of a group that offered solutions to health care needs. For me, the health training was a means of self-support. I was able to help others and it was a stepping stone for other possibilities. It became a means to further my education and provided great satisfaction. It helped me to look into medical training after I came to the U.S. I was able to major in the field of science and eventually trained as a pharmacist. I think once I arrived in the U.S. my health care training served me with motivation to go to medical school.

> *"It is hard to explain to Americans that I actually had some sort of advanced medical training. But using the language they understand, I can simply say I was trained as an LPN, but I can also say I received an extensive training while I was not even fluent in the English language. I was trained to perform certain medical procedures that were needed for that place in that time."*

The health care training may have been the gate to another world. It was a path to better opportunities. In many ways, the health care training served as a steppingstone for moving up the economic ladder. To make the long story short, the first year of my training was at Deder Hospital. Then, I was asked to consider the second year of training in the city of Nazareth, about 400 kilometers away from my hometown of Deder. As soon as I completed my training and passed the national exam (State Board), I was hired at Deder Hospital in my hometown.

Joining the Workforce

I got my first real job when Deder Hospital hired me as a lab and X-ray technician. I was responsible for the following: many sorts of blood tests, such as testing for hemoglobin; reading siderite; white and red blood cell counts; identifying malaria; and identifying other infectious blood diseases. In the lab, I was also responsible for identifying, through a microscope, any bacterial-based infections, which are common to causing tropical diseases.

The highlight from the lab experience was when the doctor I was working with then (Dr. Burkholder) and I pulled an all-nighter to do a blood transfusion (an old system known as cross tabulation), in order to save the life of an old man. He was losing blood because of hemorrhaging from his abdomen. He happened to be a good family friend who lived in the same town. The blood transfusion worked and we found a match for him so that he could get a couple of pints of blood from one of his relatives. This was an amazing experience for me.

During the same four years that I worked at Deder Hospital, I was also the X-ray technician and performed all functions of X-rays and developed all films so that the results were ready for the doctor to read. It was not unusual for me and my five friends, who completed the same training, to also scrub and assist the doctor in performing major surgeries. For example, we scrubbed to assist in the removal of abdominal tumors and helped with C-sections, appendectomies, colostomies, the repair of hernias, limb amputations, and the fixing of compound fractures after car accidents.

We did pretty much everything that is done in any general hospital or health facility. As the saying goes, in a country of the blind a one-eyed man is a king. In those days, since my country did not have enough people trained in the medical field, we filled the gap where we were needed.

Major Family Event: A New Home for My Parents

During my four years of working at the Deder Hospital, I was able to help my family in more meaningful ways. For example, I built a new house at a new location for my parents. I also bought another house for my older sister, Tadelech, which was adjacent to our new house. Additionally, I supported my brothers and sisters by paying their school fees. To this day, it continues to amaze me how I was able to save enough money at that young age and that I was able to think of real estate investment.

For me, the joy I experienced in helping family members was beyond words. After only a couple of years at my new job, at an early age, when most adolescents did not, and still do not, think beyond the self, I had this unusual capacity to help others and focus on my goals. My sister, Mismake, who was in Indianapolis recently for medical reasons, reminded me (and explained to her daughter, who was also there) that I was responsible for my siblings' education—as they put it, I paid for books, clothing and more when she and my younger brothers were in grade school. Of course, I thanked my sister for her compliment, but this type of behavior is partly an expectation of our culture. For some reason, at that age, my desire was never to be rich or to focus on myself; instead, my interest at that point was only to make a difference in the lives of my family members.

My Business Experiment

I decided to start my own business by purchasing a rural area drug store and/or clinic. I became self-employed. I was not really sure what I was getting into, but the unknown always intrigued me.

I should first say that, looking back, this was more of a service project for me than a business (for profit) experience.

Some of my friends, who went through the same medical assistance training, started opening up their own businesses (drug stores) in order to provide preventive medicine and to make money in the process. For some people I know who went in this direction, it turned out to be a lucrative business experience for them. Almost all of my friends who were in this business started making money, and some of them quickly became very wealthy.

One of my friends, who owned one of these businesses, decided to leave his business and approach me to buy it from him. I had never owned a business before and was not sure if this was what I wanted to do. I was also scared and unsure about being on my own and not having a paycheck from another source. I also knew I would be responsible for all overhead expenses. Finally, the business came with two employees for whom I was responsible. I consulted with a couple of people about this possibility. They very much encouraged me to own a business, so I took the offer.

According to government regulation, when a person started this kind of business, known as a clinic, a medical doctor had to sign on and supervise the clinic.

Under the blessing of Deder Hospital, I started my own clinic with close supervision from the medical director. The doctor made a couple of site visits a year and I also returned to the hospital so I could order supplies and receive consolation and updates. In the process, I referred patients to the hospital, and sometimes I went there with the patients.

Soon after I took ownership of the business, I discovered that I was not ready to go to my new job right away. I asked my good friend, Shawle Wehibe, who had just completed his sophomore year in high school and was looking for a summer job, to help me out. At the same time he would be fulfilling his service learning requirement. Of course, the job came with all expenses paid for, including room and board, and a mule to ride back and forth. Shawle kindly agreed and went to the town of Soka to run the clinic on my behalf for three months during his summer vacation. Since Shawle and I had the same medical training, he was certified to run the clinic and provide preventive medicine to the villagers.

At the end of the summer break, when Shawle left and went back to school, I resigned from my job at the hospital and moved to the village of Soka to work at the clinic. I was encouraged by the financial report I received from Shawle and his overall positive experience; these things affirmed my move. However, for a host of reasons, including the fact that I was young, I was still nervous and was not one-hundred percent sure if this was what I wanted to do for the rest of my life.

Even though there was a service component to it, the main thrust was to be a good businessman and make a profit. There were many poor people who were unable to pay for a couple of pain pills for the minor pains they may have been experiencing. Even though this was an economic system without a credit system, I believed health care must be available to all who needed it. So, if someone came to get some help but couldn't afford it, they got what they needed anyway. That was the way I was taught to do the job.

During my two years in the remote village, I decided to teach myself how to type. I decided that I would not go to high school before I could type. Knowing all of my academic shortcomings, I decided to equip myself with the appropriate tools to help me with school work. I was told what the academic expectations were in private schools, so I was preparing myself ahead of time in case I decided to go back to school.

I bought a small, used Olivetti typewriter and a how-to book to teach me how to type. Additionally, I invited some of my good friends and my brothers, who were in high school, to come and visit me during the summer and semester breaks in order to teach me algebra. By that point, my younger brother Teshome had graduated from high school, my second youngest brother Solomon had just finished ninth grade, and Shawle was a senior in high school.

This went on for two years, and although I was making money right and left, I was not impressed at all. It was a good life so to speak, but for some reason I was not happy just making money. The work was fun and I was well-liked by the small town people in Soka, but I felt there was something missing and the void was unbearable. My family was happy for me and thought that I was settled and that I was going to be a rich man in the family. I could have been that, but that was not what I had in my mind.

At a young age, I felt I had plenty of money in the bank, and plenty of money to support family members and relatives for a little while, at least until the next sibling finished school and took over my place.

A Desire to Know More

I was a very curious and competitive person and was eager to learn. I just knew there was something missing in my life. I felt that perhaps a high school diploma could be this missing thing, though I was not entirely sure where the road would lead.

I did not know for sure what I wanted to do, and at that point, going to college was not a pressing agenda for me, nor did I have any information about college. I also had no idea what to study in college. The college concept was too foreign to my thinking and was not on my radar at that point in time. There was no one from our family who'd gone to college. It was a foreign thought and I really did not know enough to make sense of the idea. My energy was used to do what I did best then, in the present.

Since I dropped out of school after six grades, I had a strong desire to go back to school. I knew then that I was in the wrong place, and that what I was doing did not bring me happiness. If money was the reason for starting a business, then that was an accomplishment, but it did not give me happiness. I wanted to go back to school and for some reason I thought I could matriculate at the tenth grade level. Many of my friends thought I was talking crazy, becoming grandiose and unreasonable.

I was reminded by many of my friends and family members to think through this plan. They advised me against it because they just did not see the possibility of me going from sixth grade to tenth grade. My response was that I was self-taught enough to be able to pass the eighth grade government placement exam. If I passed that test, I would give my plan a try. To me, it sounded reasonable, because I was preparing myself to go to high school during the two years I spent running a business. I am not sure if this was simply a desire to learn or if I was driven by ambition.

I was reading a lot and doing some beginning high school math. Maybe I wanted to catch up with my younger brothers, or maybe I felt I was running out of time and therefore wanted to take the chance and give it a try. So, I did.

How I went through school was unusual and ambitious. I skipped the seventh, eighth and ninth grades. I don't consider myself to be a genius, but I know that I was curious, emotionally driven to work hard, and open to risk-taking. I always thought the future was bright and that there would be an opportunity for me if I was patient and if I tried. As my father taught me, never say "I can't," but always say, "I will try."

I was well aware that it would not be easy to just jump into tenth grade if I was accepted in school. However, since I had already passed the government's national high school entrance examination while working a couple years back, I was confident that I could succeed in high school. Well, to my surprise, I took the qualifying entrance examination for tenth grade and was accepted at the Bible Academy, a Mennonite Missionary-run high school in Nazareth, Ethiopia. I must say that it was a reputable, highly desired, competitive private school. It was also small. There were 120 students when I was there, which grew to 500 by the mid-80s.

The Bible Academy

The Bible Academy was a four-year, highly selective private boarding high school. The school was very expensive and was mainly for very rich people from Addis and other parts of Ethiopia. Most families had to have wealth to send their children there for school, unless their children were offered some kind of scholarship.

Most of the youth that came to the Bible Academy were from big cities, and they were well-prepared academically to face the school's challenges. They came from families of business people, army generals, high-ranking government workers, nobles and landlords. During weekends, either parents would pick up their children to take them home or a chauffeur would be sent to pick them up and take them home.

Growing up, these young adolescents were used to watching Sesame Street on Saturday mornings in their homes. They watched western movies on weekends and were relatively well-informed about western culture. They spoke better English than those of us coming from the countryside.

Most of the youth who went to the Bible Academy turned out to be engineers, medical doctors, business owners, professors, managers, and leaders in higher education systems, both here in the States and in Ethiopia.

Despite the economic gap and class differences between rich and poor students, we got along very well. To this day, the Bible Academy is where my most memorable high school experiences took place. Most of my best and lifetime friends came from the Bible Academy. In July of 2009 we celebrated the school's 50th anniversary (the first ever school reunion) and close to 300 people showed up, including our former missionary teachers. Mr. Chester Wanger, the founder of the Bible Academy, who is now in his 90's, was present at the reunion.

I maintained confidence and motivation while in school, even though the academic work was hard for me. I was prepared to face whatever was in front of me. Since I had enough money in the bank to pay for school for several years, I decided to invest in my education. I was at the point where no one could persuade me otherwise.

Going back to school was an adjustment. I was highly motivated, exceptionally focused, and willing to do whatever it took to succeed. However, even my parents were not in support of my decision to move away from a lucrative business. I remember my father asking me this question: "Isn't the ultimate goal of going to school to get a good-paying job like what you have now, and to support yourself and family?" From his perspective he asked the right question. For him, it was a sense of loss, because he wanted to protect both me and my business. Perhaps he felt I was making a big mistake, as most fathers do. My father felt that I had all the education I needed at that time. He simply wanted me to be happy with what I had and to enjoy life.

I, however, was driven by what I call "the unknown." Maybe subconsciously there was something missing, or perhaps, I was not interested in making money. Maybe I just didn't know the reason why. What I knew was that I was driven and nothing would stop me from going back to school.

I had been out of touch with the regular classroom experience for a total of 6 years, due to my preparation for going back to school and the time it took me to accumulate enough money in the bank.

Even though I had to support myself, I was confident and comfortable with my decision. Emotionally, I was ready to tackle whatever came my way. I always believed that I was never alone, and that I had resources around me to help me reach my destination.

Reality Check

Now it was time to face reality. Some things were imagined, some expected, and some more than what I planned for. Because I escaped so many grades, academic work was challenging, as expected. The simple fact that I skipped three grades meant that I missed some of the fundamentals. It boiled down to simply working harder and studying more than other students. In tenth grade, I particularly struggled with math and physics. However, I did well in biology, chemistry and the rest of the classes. I was good enough in science that at the end of my senior year, I and only one other student, by the name of Derege, were the only two students out of 22 who qualified to take the Chemistry government placement (entrance to the university) examination.

A typical school day for me involved getting up at 4:00 AM and studying. I had to read more and review materials multiple times, and also finish homework before everyone else was even up for breakfast. Now, I wonder if a self-motivated American child would get up at 4:00 AM to study. I know my children did not do that. Getting them up for breakfast before heading out to school was a major challenge on its own. I can't even imagine my own sons being occupied with their homework during the normal hours without being reminded to do so by me or their mother.

The weekend was no different for me while I was in school. I wanted to prove to myself that I could succeed in achieving my goal, which was to finish high school. At this stage of my life I was not thinking of going to college. I was not preparing myself for college at all. I had to focus and channel all of my energy into finishing high school. I wanted to have closure for what I was currently working on. I decided to finish high school first, and then I would consider thinking about college and what that means going forward.

What helped me achieve my goals more than anything else was self-confidence and trusting myself. I believed in trying new things, checking things out, and asking for help when necessary. I believed that some people knew more than others about a particular thing only because they were exposed to what they knew ahead of others.

I always believed that I was no less intelligent than others, and that I could do whatever I set my mind to. I knew how to ask for help when I needed it, and I believed it was okay to understand one's limits. However, I was one of those people who could rise to the occasion if need be.

Looking back, I must have had well-developed cognitive, social and emotional skills. I was able to adapt to a new environment quickly, and I was able to develop networks to my advantage. I connected with good students on campus and became a student leader. I also became friends with students who were mature and happy to be in school, and avoided those who were there to please their parents. There were a handful of mature, older students who'd chosen to come to the school to learn, and they made my life very easy. Actually, I was part of a contingent of older and mature students with previous work experience.

In order to support myself, I did continue to work while in school. I lined up weekend and vacation jobs at the local Mission (Mennonite-run hospital). I was also hired at the high school as a school nurse.

Unexpected Interruption from School

Another temptation was to go back to the work world. After only one year in high school, at the end of tenth grade, I was contacted by Daniel Sensing, a missionary and a good friend of my father. He simply informed me about a new organization called All African Leprosarium Rehabilitation and Training Center (AALRT) in Addis Ababa. He told me that this organization was looking for an X-ray technician and medical photographer for the summer.

I applied and took the job for that summer, and the assignment ended up lasting for one year. While I was at AALRT, I was told that there was a possibility for the organization to send me to Sweden for more training in medical photography. This made me decide not to go back to the Bible Academy for eleventh grade. This is where I made mistakes and did not think of any long-term consequences.

I also thought that I could possibly work during the day and go to school at night to finish high school. Well, it was not that simple. The one year with the organization was good enough for me. I knew I was not going anywhere, even to Sweden, until I finished high school. At this point, the only option left for achieving my goal was to go back to the Bible Academy to finish high school. I learned that a shortcut may work sometimes, but it wasn't going to work out this time.

The highlight of this part of my journey was the experience of living with my brother Teshome and my sister Mismake in an apartment in Addis Ababa. My mother hired a maid for us from Deder and sent her to live with us and help us with cooking and cleaning. Mismake was attending high school and Teshome was working for an insurance company in Addis Ababa. That was a wonderful arrangement. At this time, life was so good that Teshome and I tried to buy a 1950 Chevy without thinking about upkeep and maintenance. I don't think we had much in savings in our bank account that we could've used to deal with an old American car. Thank God it did not happen.

I decided to go back to the Bible Academy to complete my third and fourth years. After these additional two years at the Bible Academy, I was done and ready for another challenge. As I mentioned earlier, all through high school I secured a job for weekends and during summer vacations at the local Mennonite hospital. This allowed me to earn money. The health training I'd received earlier became a wonderful opportunity for finding a job. I served at the school health center as a nurse, and this also helped me to earn some extra cash. Compared to other students from my region, I was comfortable and always had some spending money. As I indicated earlier, most of my classmates who attended the Bible Academy came from well-to-do families and they did not need to work to support themselves at all.

Working in Addis Ababa

After graduating from high school, I was blessed with an unexpected opportunity for work in Addis. A pharmaceutical import and export company (St. Gabriel Pharmacy), owned by the family of one of my classmates (the Mehari family), invited me to oversee the day-to-day activities of the main wholesale department and the pharmacy. In some ways, I was sort of like a manager of their business in Addis Ababa. This was a dream job for me, because I got to stay with the Mehari family, and because the position came with room and board and a car. This was very unusual and I consider it a blessing. I can say this was one of the best experiences in my young adult life. The friendships and relationships I developed are still intact to this day. To this day, the entire Mehari family continues to be a very special family with whom I stay in touch and I try visit some of them when I can.

While at St. Gabriel, I was responsible for the inventory of the warehouse. I was trusted to be the point person to open and close the pharmacy store and the main wholesale department. In the beginning of my assignment I did inventory of supply and oversaw the shipment of drugs to the countryside. Salesmen came in and out of our store. I was in charge of making sure that all the vehicles were serviced and in working order. When the owner, Gashe Mehari, was out of the country, I was simply in charge of the day-to-day functions of a well-known and highly respected multi-million dollar business.

While I was in Addis Ababa, I developed a focused interest on going to college. This may have been the result of being exposed to too many college-bound students in Addis Ababa, and to some extent a function of my own development. Communicating with Shawle, who was already at Hesston College, may have triggered more interest, prompting me to further consider whether I should go to college.

My plan was to work in Addis for a year and in the meantime prepare to come to the United States to go to college. Just before I made arrangements to come to Hesston College, I was responsible for passing the TOEFL exam and fulfilling other governmental requirements. I was also responsible for providing payment plans to the college. The college awarded me a full tuition grant for two years, but I had to be responsible for my room and board. Shawle and Mary Jane introduced me to Liz Hunsberger, who was a Hesston College faculty member at the time. After communicating with Liz for about six months, she offered me significant support for room and board while I was at Hesston. I am grateful to Professor Liz Hunsberger for contributing to my college education. I saw Liz during the Mennonite World Conference in Harrisburg, PA in 2015, where we both agreed that her investment in my education was not in vain.

As part of my preparation for traveling to America for college, I took TOEFL and passed, was processed for my passport, and stayed in touch with Shawle and Mary Jane. As you may have guessed by now, Shawle and Mary Jane were very instrumental in my coming to the States. They encouraged me to prepare for college and complete the proper paperwork from Hesston College with the help of the international student advisor.

I was fortunate that things worked out well for me in Addis at the Meharis'. After a year of working at Gabriel Pharmacy in Addis, I'd saved almost enough money for my plane ticket and secured my student visa. I was ready to move to another country in order to receive a college education. Almost all the planning in terms of the necessary preparation to travel abroad for college took place in that one year while I was in Addis.

Attending college in Ethiopia would have been another option, but the chance of being accepted at the Addis Ababa University was very small because they could only admit 4,500 students each fall. The number of students who finished high school and were ready to go to a university was at least 10,000 to 15,000 every year. Therefore, many smart students had no opportunity to pursue their educational goals. The competition was very steep and I was not up to it. Addis Ababa University was a place for financially well-to-do and connected people, and I was not from that club.

Part III: Coming to America for Education

The Decision that Changed My Life

I remember it well as if it was just yesterday. While working in Addis for a year, I saved all that I could (as I mentioned) and yet I was about $400 short for my plane ticket and other incidentals. This is just the beginning finance related college orientation. The point here is that I decided to go to college without totally knowing exactly what I need to do now and when I go to the United States, in terms of the academic challenges, finances, and cultural adjustment. However, I decided to make it work and I wasn't going to give up. I worked the whole year and saved everything I could, but what I saved was not enough to purchase the plane ticket to fly from Ethiopia to America. The big question for me was, what could I do now?

Shawle and Mary Jane sent me $200 (remember, he was a college student), but then I was still $200 short. None of my other relatives could lend me the money I needed toward purchasing my ticket. Some friends I had also told me they didn't have that kind of money sitting around. So, I went to the person I was working for. I went to Gashe Mehari and told him what I was dealing with. After he listened to my story, he simply said to me, "Zenebe, just hand me what you have and I will take care of the rest and you will have your plane ticket." He sounded like he had done this before to help someone else, and it did not take him long to respond. He did not tell me he needed time to think about it. Right on the spot, as if I was one of his sons, he told me he would help me. He also said to me, "I know you are going to be a help to someone someday. I will help you purchase your ticket." He added, "You are going to America for a college education." What a relief that was! To this day I recall what Gashe Mehari said to me as if it happened yesterday.

I promised to repay him the money within two years. He purchased the ticket for me to come to the States. In less than 18 months I had saved enough money from campus work to repay Gashe Mehari what I owed him, and the rest is history. This was a remarkable and yet unexpected and shocking event for me, however, all worked out well in my favor.

What was ironic about all of this is that in about five years, this wealthy man who had everything and more and responded to my crisis when I needed him, was suddenly under duress because of the revolution and lost most of what he owned. I can't even begin to explain what happened during the Marxist revolution in my country. First of all, I wasn't there, and following the events from a distance was very different at that time. It was a major upheaval and more than a simple matter of many families losing their wealth, though that also happened to many people unfairly. Most of all, thousands lost their lives during that time.

During the revolution (known as Derg), over twenty plus years, hundreds, possibly even millions, were displaced and left the country. An unknown number of Ethiopians, both for and against the government, lost their lives. Since I was not in Ethiopia during that time I can't say anything more with certainty. What I stated here was what I read about and what I was told. I may have left out most of the worst part of the twenty years of the revolution in Ethiopia.

One day, out of the blue, I got a phone call from my friend Gashe Mehari, the man who made it possible for me to come to America. He said, "Please, I need your help! Please help me get my youngest son out of Ethiopia. The situation here is going from bad to worse. I would like to see my youngest son moved to a safe place and I would like to see him go to the States for a college education. Would you please find a way to assist me in finding my son a college he can be admitted to, particularly at the college where you work?" I remember the phone conversation with Gashe Mehari very well and how I was so glad that he contacted me. I was honored by the request and I was so glad I was in the position to positively respond to my dear friend, the person who made a difference in my life when I needed his help in 1972.

So, yes, I was able to assist his son in coming to Hesston College for his education. It was with great joy that I wanted to assist Gashe Mehari as he helped me when I was in need of his assistance. This kind of thoughtful human response and compassion to one another reminds me of a Bible verse found in Matthew 7:12: "So in everything, do to others what you would have them do to you, for thus sums up the Law and the Prophets."

Hesston College

I arrived on American soil on August 12, 1972. I came in as F-1 Student visa, so I was legal. My two years at Hesston College provided me with the most rewarding and fascinating experience. I had a God-sent roommate from Pennsylvania named John Sharp; as well as Arland Eash, who invited me to his home for my first Christmas in the U.S. and of course, Ron Blaum, who kindly lent me use his car to drive so I can visit my brother in Illinois. As a foreign student, one could not ask for a better match for a roommate. Of course, cultural adjustment was a challenge. The homesickness, language problems and general adjustment to the overall American culture were beyond challenging.

My first impression of Americans at Hesston was one of kindness, helpfulness and interest. At Hesston, the professors and the people in the community were very accepting and friendly. I found them to be hardworking, good people who had an interest in genuinely helping others. They liked to assist foreign students by providing transportation and taking them to their churches and their homes for holidays. Most Americans were all good and more. However, this goodwill did not last long and very soon things changed. A clear message was sent that the honeymoon was over. The expectation was that foreign students needed to find ways to stand on their own feet as soon as possible.

In many ways, for foreign students, this message was a good reminder to hold on to what we call "our own," such as language, culture, family and other aspects from our home land. These cultural resources we brought with us should have quickly helped us adjust in our new environment. Furthermore, we came to this country willingly with the sole purpose of attending college, so we should have been ready to do that. Generally speaking, foreign students were also grateful for the support and the good orientation we received from the host country. This should have enabled us to focus on our education. However, when crossing national boundaries, no one can escape the inevitable challenge of cultural shock.

I included a number of significant images to help me tell my story.
My Ethiopian family. Not pictured is my brother Tamene.

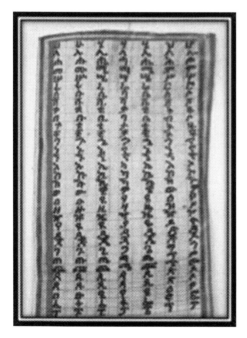

The Ethiopian alphabet known as "Fedel"

My high school friends

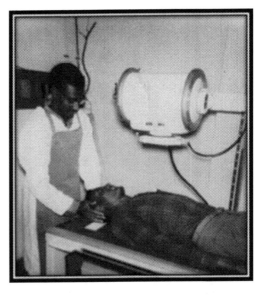

Zenebe as an X-ray Technician

On the Hesston College soccer team

Zenebe on Hesston College track team

Barbara and Zenebe's Wedding August 19, 1979

My Mom, Barbara, and my Dad in Goshen in 1984

With friends at my graduation from Southern Illinois University

Kaleab, Zenebe and Ashe at Westminster Bridge in London, July 3, 1998

Our home for 5 years in Fresno, California

December 2003 Christmas in California

Our new home in Indianapolis.

Zenebe with Grandchildren, June 2015

Zenebe and Mismake in the hospital

Mismake in the hospital, surrounded by her brothers

Tadelech, Gedamu, Zenebe, Teshome, and Gedamu's wife Mentiwab in Awasa during our December, 2011 visit to Ethiopia

Young Abebe family in North Manchester

The top picture shows my dear sister Mismake, Surafel and Sisay.
The bottom picture is of Mimake with her younger brothers Tamene and Sisay.

The 2015 Abebe Reunion

For the first time, the Abebe boys met the MCC man, Menno Chupp, who built their two-room school house in Ethiopia. (July 2015)

The Five CEOs in the MCC U.S. System in 2015. Nathan Yoder, Michelle Armster, Bruce Compbell-Janz, Ron Byler and Zenebe Abebe

Deder - Zenebe's Birth Place

Cultural Shock

Through all these ups and downs during my time of adjustment, known as cultural shock, I found myself wondering why I did not have more meaning in my life. The time of picture-taking and sending to family members is now over. In other words, the honeymoon is over and the old way of life is now changing. I repeatedly have to tell myself that I am really away from home.

The feeling of being away from home and family members is just setting in. All of a sudden, I felt out of place. People acted strangely and behaved differently and I was not interested in them. I thought, "they look different, act different, and think different." I found them to be uncaring and uninterested.

The absence of my family, and the feeling of not belonging, made me even more willing to say that I was indeed an Ethiopian. This was how I felt; I did not like what I was experiencing. The main challenge for me was cultural conflict and the human behavior in this strange land. I was locked in and had nowhere to go. I had to make it work.

I knew I was in America, but not yet an American in every sense of the word. Of course, at the time, my observation was that Americans behaved differently, as they should, and yet it appeared that we had nothing in common. They were more free and uninhibited. They seemed to be much more unaware of the world around them, as if America was their whole world. To me, it seemed the sense of community was missing, and that individualism was what was important to everyone around me.

I was troubled to my core by this foreign land and its people. I was simply missing my home and family and my people. I was missing the sounds and voices of family members. This is simply to say that the sounds and voices from home were certainly not forgotten, but they were far away. I dreamt of my family night after night, and then the morning would come and I would discover that it had only been a dream, and that my family was nowhere to be seen. I missed the faces of my dad and mom. I missed my family, all of them, like I had never missed anyone in my life before. I missed the holidays, I missed the food, and I missed speaking the Amharic language. No American jokes made me laugh, and no one ever smiled at my jokes. I was totally disconnected and even lost. The only things that gave me hope were the three to four week-old handwritten letters I received from Ethiopia. The once-a-month phone calls from Shawle or Teshome were like Christmas gifts. I think I was depressed (reactive depression). I could not sleep well and did not eat well. However, I could see a trace of hope and meaning in my journey to the United States.

On the other hand, I knew why I was at Hesston, and that I wanted to finish college no matter the challenge. I quickly figured out that I needed more connection with the people in this foreign land. I needed to make friends and to trust people, even when I thought we had nothing in common.

In many ways, politically and socially speaking at that time, America was being defined by the Civil Rights movement, racism, the sexual revolution, drugs, and the influx of immigrants coming from other countries.

It was a time when members of American society were trying to define who they were and who they wanted to become. Through it all, I was at times confused, and yet also felt privileged to be defining myself in the midst of these changes. Change was taking place all around me in this unfamiliar land.

One thing that was very interesting to me was that America was unique, like nowhere else in the world, and anyone could become part of the American experience. In actuality, it may not have felt this way to all people, and it may not have happened this way for all people, but the spirit and the opportunity were there for anyone who wished to be part of this welcoming nation.

What Sustains Us?

Here, I am speaking on behalf of my brothers and other Ethiopian immigrant students. Being away from your family and culture for an extended period of time at a younger age is not easy. I sometimes wondered: what kept us going? I must say that as glamorous as it sounds to travel abroad and study, it was not always fun and had its own challenges. This was not home and this was not a friendly place all the time, so one would wonder, in this lonely place away from family and home, what really kept one going? For me, among many other things, I always kept recalling my country's history and language, and the traditions that were unique and special. I believed that for those of us living abroad, our music and holiday traditions were a couple of good Ethiopian customs that kept us all connected to our culture. Our Ethiopian tradition was filled with exceptional history, including resistance to colonialism, a unique language, the Julien calendar, and our Yaradian music. These things all gave us a unique perspective as to who we were.

Even today, in the computer age of the 21st century, I personally enjoy paying attention to what is going on in the new age of high-tech electronic media. I listen to Ethiopian music from my generation via YouTube videos. I read Ethiopian news posted daily through the Ethiopian media. This linkage helps me stay connected to what I call a special identity. This identity is what I claim as my own in a foreign land, and it keeps me going.

Today, the world has become smaller, more accessible, and even more fascinating and fun and exciting to live in. The trips I make every other year or so to Ethiopia have served me as a point of connection to my people and culture. I love the experience and am able to stay connected to what matters, including extended family, culture and tradition.

Preparedness

When traveling to another country, it may not always be possible to be one-hundred percent prepared for the unexpected. However, a thoroughly prepared person may be able to minimize the length of time it normally takes to adjust to a new culture. I consider myself to be an extrovert, but even for me, adjustment did not come as easy as I thought it would. I was never totally prepared to handle what was to come. When it comes to a social setting, or if I am interested in something, I seldom wait to be invited. Of course, this means I am willing to take the risk of being rejected, which has happened many times. I have also gained much by interacting with others even when it seemed threatening or made me feel lonely, strange and out of place. I hate to admit it but that has also happened many times. Preparing oneself for a culture which is significantly different politically, socially and in particular, linguistically is possible but not easy.

Coming to America requires a good, long preparation. Long before packing personal items, preparing oneself emotionally is the first step. Getting ready to go to an unfamiliar place requires other forms of preparation.

Here, I am talking about preparing oneself in advance to tackle the academic work that comes with learning another language (in another culture), getting used to a new way of life, and adjusting to a new space and time. Enduring all of these things, and more, requires time and patience. When crossing borders one must be prepared to tolerate the temporary inconveniences that you may possibly face.

As a college student, I learned that the social and cultural issues in a new setting could easily take over the precious time foreign students have to devote to academic work. Added to all of these adjustments, among other things, are homesickness and the issue of belonging. These are strong narratives that must be recorded for those who care about us. These emotional narratives, as important as they are, still represent a narrow slice of our life experiences. Emotions run deep when you do not have the feeling of belonging, or when you feel disconnected. The feeling of unworthiness can easily take over your emotions.

While I was at Hesston College, I was welcomed and people in the community were generally kind to me on the surface. At a deep personal level, however, it was hard for some people to understand what I was experiencing. Some thought I should just be happy to be in America. If I talked about missing home, the common response was that foreign students should not complain at all. When most Americans hear about, or notice, the confusion foreign students experience because of cultural shock or home sickness, they simply tend to play it down with statements such as, 'foreign students should just be happy that they are here and they should just be happy and enjoy the American life.' At least at that time, since most of our college friends have no travel experience abroad and they cannot relate to what we are talking about.

From my experience, the issue of trying to make it in a foreign land without the encouraging voices of family and friends was a challenge. In other words, being away from family and friends was hard to get used to. Shawle and Mary Jane (Steve was only 2 years old then) had already moved to Goshen, Indiana. My brother, Teshome, and his wife, Asegedech, lived in Normal, Illinois and were going to school at Illinois State University, so they were about 300 miles away.

The first year at Hesston College went fine for me. The second year, I was more involved in my own learning. I became more involved in campus life. I was more social and a bit more understanding and accepting of my situation. I understood that this was the way it was going to be, and that I would have to make the best of it.

I was asked to be a Resident Assistant, which was a challenge on its own. I did that, played soccer, joined the track team, and was asked to join an outreach team as well. This made me extremely busy, and even made my time at Hesston more enjoyable. My efforts to connect with people paid off. After two years at Hesston, I was set to go off to another Mennonite College, this one in Indiana.

Goshen College

Moving from Hesston to Goshen College in Goshen, Indiana was a big step forward for me. My experience as a student at Goshen College and within the community was short and was not as eventful as my experience at Hesston. I was more studious at Goshen and focused on going to grad school after graduation. I took only a year to finish the academic program at Goshen College. So, within three years of my arrival in the States, I earned a degree in Psychology.

Before I continue discussing my time at Goshen, I should explain why I didn't return to Ethiopia after I completed my degree in Psychology. As I mentioned briefly towards the beginning of this memoir, my original plan was to go back to Ethiopia for good as soon as I earned my bachelor's degree from Goshen College. Unfortunately, in 1974, a Marxist government overthrew Emperor Haileselasse, which ended the Monarchy. Going back to Ethiopia became unthinkable for a while. The only way my brother Teshome and I could stay in the U.S. was on a work visa or a student visa. Since we did not have a work visa, we decided to be professional students until the situation changed in our country. So, I decided to continue my education all the way until I completed my Ph.D.

The campus and enrollment of Goshen College were much larger than those at Hesston, with close to 1,300 students, about 90 percent of whom were residential. There were many international students, and maybe 5-6 Ethiopian students, which made the campus tolerable. Since this was during the Civil Rights movement, the number of African American students enrolled was about 70-80, and almost all of them came from inner city areas and were part of a special governmental program that afforded them free tuition.

The Impact of Campus Life at Goshen College

The African American students did not find Goshen College or the surrounding community to be necessarily a friendly place. In the community, on the campus, and, ironically, in their own country, they were strangers as much as the international students.

In the early 1990's, when I was a vice president for Multicultural Education at Goshen College, we developed a program that was designed to bring former students of color (Blacks, Hispanics, Asians, and Native Americans) back to campus. We named it the "Alumni

Scholar Program." It was a grant-funded program with two main purposes:

1. To hear the stories and experiences of former students of color from Goshen College; and to educate current students about the history of the past.

2. To show them the quality of leaders that came out of the community of color.

We were able to involve the faculty by having them help identify former students who'd attended Goshen College for at least two years. Of course, most of the students who came back were graduates. We were able to attract former students who had attended Goshen College from the 50's through the 80's. They spoke at convocations/chapel and lectured in classrooms. Some spoke in small group settings and also consulted with faculty and administrators.

In about a four to six year period, we brought back over 30 Goshen College graduates who were persons of color. By the time they returned, they were dentists, physicians, nurses, social workers, professors, teachers, pastors, businessmen and businesswomen from all over the country. They were happy to be invited back and they were very willing and ready to share their stories.

When they discussed their Goshen College experiences, almost every one of the speakers highlighted the strong academic programs from which they benefited. Some also mentioned a faculty member or two, who had served them as a mentor or with whom they'd been good friends. However, almost all of them also spoke about a campus that was unfriendly and racist toward them. They indicated how lonely they felt, and how they were distanced from everyone else. They mentioned that in any social settings on campus, white students and staff alike did not care about their presence. Some didn't even acknowledge them. If they were involved in any sports, they were praised for their good performance. As bad as it sounded, and as unacceptable as it was, they said they chose to take the high road and simply tolerated what was coming at them because they wanted to get a good education.

For almost all of the alumni scholars, this was their first return to the campus since graduation. Despite the good educations they received, they left Goshen College and the larger community with feelings of anger and resentment. They left with no intention of returning to their alma mater. Through the years, only a handful of alumni of color (mostly international) enrolled their children at Goshen College.

While at Goshen College, My Student Days Experience at Goshen, I worked as a student on campus to financially support myself and pay some of my school expenses. I worked at four different jobs, including at the physical plant (maintenance), switchboard, library, and audio visual department.

During my 4th year in the United States (after the completion of my Psychology degree), I was assigned to do an internship at Elkhart General Hospital in the Psychiatric Unit for one year as part of my psychology training. It was a good time for me to determine which area of psychology I wanted to pursue in graduate school, and also a good time to take the GRE for the following academic year. For me, it was a year to start sending application forms to different graduate schools and to look at their programs. During this one year, my situation changed and I saved some money and purchased a used car (VW). I was beginning to feel comfortable and almost started to develop a sense of belonging. This positioned me to establish a credit in this borrow-and-spend system.

As a student at Goshen College I was not involved much in extracurricular activities because I was working many hours to meet my financial obligation. I was also focusing on going to graduate school, so I decided to spend more time studying than doing anything else.

Northern Illinois University

As I stated above, after graduating from Goshen College, in order to fulfill a psychology major requirement, I was asked to participate in an internship at Elkhart General Hospital in the Psychiatric Unit.

I believe my attendance at Northern Illinois University was a result of my Elkhart General Hospital internship experience. Another reason had to do with Teshome and Asegedech going to graduate school at Northern. I joined the Community Mental Health (Allied Health Profession) Counseling, two-year, Master's Program. Of course, I was awarded a graduate assistantship, which paid for my tuition and fees. At that time, I considered this to be an opportunity of a lifetime, since I was a young adult who came to this country with no money to speak of but was now attending graduate school and even had a car to help with my transportation needs. My attitude at that time was that I was happy, not much more to ask for and I had a lot to be thankful about.

The academic program, the faculty, and the overall environment made my experience very enjoyable. Additionally, Teshome and his family, and a number of Ethiopian students were also there, so I had a good support system in place. Northern, of course, was the place where Barbara and I met.

During my second year at Northern Illinois University, I met my lovely wife, Barbara Stewart, from Memphis, TN. It was the winter of 1977. She introduced herself to me as a resident from Chicago, but Barbara was really from down south; she had the southern accent. Since I was relatively new to the country, I had no idea what the significance of the north and south division was all about. Since I came from across the ocean, that was the most pronounced cultural and linguistic difference I paid attention to.

As the saying goes those who are educated must teach; I came from Ethiopia equipped with a driving license, but Barbara lived in the American city of Memphis without a driving license. I thought everyone in America owned a car and, of course, carried a driving license. Somehow I assumed that when young adults complete high school they are required to get a driving license. Well, it came as a surprise to me that Barbara did not have one. Right away, I put on my mission hat and started my contribution to American society – I offered Barbara driving lessons.

My First Job

It is a long story, but about six month after Barbara and I met, I graduated from Northern. I had a job offer at a community counseling center in Rockford, Illinois to work as a counselor/therapist. I did all the paperwork and signed an acceptance letter for employment in Rockford. I was all ready to move to the city, and was even in the process of looking for a place to live, when I received a call from Goshen College offering me a position to serve as the Director of Residence Hall (RD) and to teach in the Psychology Department. It was a hard decision, but I called Rockford and told them I was sorry, but that I had accepted another position and was now moving to Goshen, Indiana.

Working at Mennonite Colleges/Universities

I thought it would be good for me to go back to a familiar place to work. I was excited to be invited back and eager to do my best at my job. The first year was a difficult experience. I don't even know how I did it, but somehow I managed.

This was a time period where racism was at its peak and it was literally the law of the land. Unfortunately, in many southern states, black people were treated as property and not as humans. It was a time where black people were fighting for their constitutional rights, while white people were fighting for their privileges and trying to protect their white supremacy. One can only imagine the confusion and social disruption the country was experiencing.

I spent twenty-eight years in Mennonite, and Mennonite-related, higher learning institutions, and about eighteen of those years at Goshen College. I am fortunate to have had the opportunity to work at these institutions. They allowed me to make a living and raise my family, and they provided me with the opportunity to develop socially, personally and professionally. As a family, we were enriched by church members and people we met in the communities. I think this is where our children call home because this is where they grew up and made the most of what was there for them. We lived with good people in the community and we made many friends. Even with all of its challenges, we always claimed the community we lived in as our own and we made it work for us.

This was not an inviting community. There were some people who did not like seeing people of color in Goshen. As we learned, there is a lot to be said about the trailblazers in Goshen who were here before us. Some tolerated the situation and lived there for a while, and others wanted nothing to do with this unfriendly place and its people and they simply packed up and left soon after arrival.

I am also grateful for those people of color who lived in this community. By tolerating the situation, they made Goshen their home before us. In many ways, they paved the way for us. Some of these people we knew, and some we did not know, although we heard their stories. We stood on the shoulders of many African American men and women who paid the price of racism and were not welcomed into these communities. Even though I learned about the original American sin (racism) before coming to the United States, I was not at all prepared for the vicious, unearned, and collective institutional power and privilege of white people. I was not equipped to deal with it at all, because I did not know how. My church experience did not provide me with a framework to process and respond to this madness. The issues of institutional racism I am talking about here is not only a thing of the past, even today it remains one of this country's national challenges.

There were always people who were supportive and served as allies in this world of racism. I continue to be grateful to those individuals for their prophetic voice and for joining me and others in the work against institutional racism. There were some colleagues and friends who sometimes spoke openly against institutional and individual racism, and they made the living and working environment tolerable. I came to know, and worked side by side with, some individuals who were genuinely committed and involved in the work of dismantling racism in the community.

Despite the challenges I mentioned, I would like to believe that both in my workplace and in the community where we lived, my family worked hard and did our best to understand, to educate, to accommodate, to disagree, and to confront others when we had to.

Most of all, as a family, we decided to take the high road and collaborate with our white brothers and sisters everywhere we lived and worked in order to contribute toward a better future.

From Northern Illinois to Goshen College

Each place I lived in, either alone or with my family, came with its own unique challenges. I thought it would be good for me to go back to a familiar place to work. I was excited to be invited back to Goshen and eager to do my best at my job. The first year was a difficult experience. I don't even know how I did it, but I managed. This was in the late 70s, as I mentioned, when racism was at its peak and the Civil Rights movement was surging forward at full throttle.

It was, and still is, amazing to me how white people, young and old, rich and poor, could have the same mindset. They were socialized not to respect black people as equal human beings. In fact, the city of Goshen, as reported in the *Mennonite World Review* on April 27, 2015, had a sundown post, which meant Goshen City residents and the city tried to maintain Goshen as a nearly all-white population for at least the first two-thirds of the 20th century.

This type of understanding in the city and the larger community, including the college campus, was passed on to the younger generation of whites as a way of life in order to help them protect the privilege that came with white skin.

Sometimes, looking back, I wonder how in the world I became a director of a residence hall of students who had never learned how to respect persons of color. These were the students with no knowledge of history, who had no idea where I came from. They had no idea that Ethiopia was the only country on the continent of Africa that had not been colonized by whites.

These students had no concept of my experiences with white people growing up. For me, and for my people, "white" translated to mean colonialists, fascists, invaders and Europeans.

I strongly believe that because of my upbringing and culture, my attitude was that I was in charge and the students were to follow the rules of the college. I was firm and yet respectful toward anyone who followed the rules. I had no tolerance for anyone who exhibited a racist attitude, or who chose to not respect themselves and others. I was ready to educate and change the minds of those who followed white supremacist ideology. For sure, the experience itself exposed me to emotional wounding, but I was able to tolerate the situation enough to live with it for a while. I believed that over time things would change for the better. And yet, in 2015 things seem to be regressing to where we were in the 70's.

Mono Culture & Menno Youth

However, in the 70's, my challenge was to introduce the students to a new culture. No matter my background, culture, language and accent, and no matter my shortcomings, I shouldered the burden of educating and leading these kids. Leading the "unleadable" was a major task. I was frustrated by too many of these unsophisticated young adults, who potentially could have ended up being leaders in this society someday.

At that time, the campus consisted of almost all white students. About 90 percent were from Mennonite churches. They were not only from farming backgrounds, but also unfamiliar with people of color. For some of these white kids, this was their first time to meet and see black students face to face. They were not only scared of blacks, but unequipped with the necessary social skills to communicate and socialize. Simple social greetings were a challenge for them. They were fearful and stayed to themselves. I was painfully made aware of the fact that a significant number of white students then, and even now, were socially inept. Even for some of the faculty and staff, their unpreparedness concerning social interactions was obvious when they had the opportunity to interact with some of the inner city black students but didn't seem to know what to do with them.

It was clear to me that real change was overdue, and that it would require not only the Goshen population to change, but for the nation as a whole to promote social change. That was back then, but the issues have not been resolved yet so there is a lot to be done going forward. That social change is necessary if the nation wants to move toward a better America that is open to viewing all humans as belonging to one nation, under God, indivisible and with liberty and justice for all. It is time for young adults of the white race to understand and practice the above stated values of this nation soon.

Back then, young adults of the white race seemed virtually unprepared for a diverse world. They got confused in social interactions, particularly with people of color. They simply looked awkward and confused by the timing. They didn't know what to do and didn't understand the importance of social interactions and simple greetings.

I became aware that these were students with no social values other than their own. They never had the opportunity to see their parents socially interact with people of color. They had not lived next door to people of color, nor did they attend church with any. They had not seen students of color in their classrooms, and they had not shared playgrounds with black people. Whites always questioned black people's ability to do anything worthwhile in society. This was the environment, the culture, which college students of that time came from.

The college students and some of their professors (my colleagues) were simply deprived of these and other social and life experiences. One could almost conclude that white young adults of that time were not only unprepared for the real world, but that something was missing in their lives that kept them from being fully functioning individuals in a setting outside of their own social context. I sometimes wonder if, as a group, they suffered from social paralysis. I believe racism, the ideology of white supremacy, and the way we deal with it on a daily basis.

When I look back, I recognize that working with this group was not easy. As I said, they'd had few interactions with people of color. In this type of an environment how can a person of color expect anything more positive from whites? Given their upbringings, ideology and belief system, some whites will take many generations to change. Even back then I knew that racism was in the making in this country for years, and I was sure it would take generations to unlearn what they'd learned for so many years.

Generally speaking, international students, on the other hand, were treated differently at Goshen College, because they were considered visitors who were there temporarily. As a result, they were not viewed as a psychological threat to the powerbase of the white system. Since I was teaching psychology classes, I heard a lot of stories from some of my white students about how they felt concerning their social unpreparedness.

I can say that I may have taken the first step in guiding the future leaders of the next generation. Years later, just as I thought would happen, I began seeing many of my former students filling leadership roles in businesses, schools, colleges/universities, and churches. Most of these students were positioned to use their networks and connections to get these jobs.

Despite the challenges and responsibilities I faced, I considered my first year of employment to be more or less a good learning experience. Additionally, the experience gave me a good start for what was to come in my 30 plus year career in higher education.

I also observed the transformations of some young adults. The light bulb turned on early for them in life so that they could clearly understand that their world would be different from their parents' world. They were open to learning and embraced the diversity of their future world. They turned out to be respectful of others and had a better understanding of God's kingdom as being inclusive of peoples of all nationalities, languages and tribes. Some turned out to be advocates of anti-racism and anti-oppression efforts in their communities.

For me, the experience simply educated me more than any classroom lecture or small group discussion I ever had about race. If I accomplished anything, it happened because of the risk I took, the difficulties I faced and the challenges I dealt with. Going through these turbulent times made me question the value of certain groups of people, helped me develop coping mechanisms and survival techniques, and helped me control situations when I could. Most of all, I learned how to survive in a racist community.

Major Family Event: My Marriage to Barbara

On August 18, 1979, Barbara and I got married in Memphis, Tennessee at Beulah Baptist Church, which was Barbara's home church. We purchased our first home in Goshen. Kaleab was born on May 1, 1981.

Life with Barbara

During my second year working at Goshen College, Barbara and I decided to get married. Since Barbara was still at Northern Illinois University and only had one more year to go, we decided she should transfer to Goshen and finish at Goshen College, where the tuition would be free after we got married. We got married on August 18, 1979. All of my brothers and close friends in the States, some of my college friends, and a number of colleagues from work made the long journey from Northern Indiana, Michigan, Pennsylvania, and Illinois to join us at our wedding in Memphis, Tennessee. While I was still working as a Resident Director of Yoder Hall, the two of us living in a college apartment, Barbara graduated from Goshen College in the spring of 1980.

During my third and last year as Resident Director at Goshen College, Barbara started working at, what was then, Salem Bank, in Goshen. She got this job with the help of our good friend John Stith. He was the only African American living in Goshen when we moved there, and he was the City Post Master General. At that time, businesses in the city of Goshen, Indiana did not hire black people. It is a long story, so we could write a book on this experience alone, but the point is that John Stith was our networking connection back then who helped Barbara secure a position at the local bank.

Kaleab was born on May 1st, 1981 at Goshen General Hospital. Because he was our first child, Kaleab was very special to us, as is the case with all first-time parents. We did everything to protect him and raise him well. We moved out of the college apartment and at the same time, I took on a different responsibility at the college as the Associate Director of the Financial Aid Office.

In the late spring of 1981, around the time Kaleab was born, Barbara and I managed to purchase our first home in Goshen, Indiana. This was a very invigorating experience. The birth of our first child was followed by our first home. Barbara's work at Salem Bank helped us with mortgage loans. The rest is history.

The house was located at 1014 South 14ᵗʰ Street, a small three bedroom, modest house with a one-car garage. The purchase price at that time was only $36,000. This was during President Reagan's administration, when the country was going through some rough times due to high unemployment, inflation and high interest rates that were out of control. Americans were falsely feeling hopeful, even when they did not have much. At that time, interest rates for financing a mortgage were at 12 percent. I learned early on that most Americans build wealth by purchasing a house, unless one expects to receive a family inheritance, which was not the case for us. I was once told that, normally, it is possible to build equity from the house through time. At least at that time, a house appreciated about 3 to 5 percent annually on average. Even now, in 2015, the chance of getting a good return in home investment is much better than if you just have money in a savings account.

After Kaleab's birth, Barbara went back to Salem Bank for a year, at which time we were asked to co-lead a Study Service Term (SST), or Study Abroad Program, in Belize, Central America. By then, Kaleab was about 18 months old.

A Brief Word about Barbara

Barbara and I were meant for each other. Her character and behavior are as beautiful as her face. I was attracted to her by her quality of kindness, impeccable character, and ability to relate to anyone. Most of all, she is gracious. She is not only kind, but once she knows you, she is, to some extent, trusting and always happy. She has the ability to always make friends. People always remember Barbara because of her ability to laugh things off, no matter the situation. Through the years, our family was blessed because of her ability to make friends and go the extra miles to accommodate others.

Barbara and I have two things in common: we both believe in hard work and supporting family members. Additionally, we both believe in sharing what we have, and we have similar thoughts when it comes to raising children. We always felt that our children saw us as their champions and their fans. We believed that our children needed us the most at a younger age, while their self-esteem, social skills, and character were all being developed. We also believed that we could only raise our children once, meaning that we couldn't go back and undo any mistakes. We believed that parenting was not about providing our children with an overwhelming amount of toys, it was about spending quality time with them. Of course, this thinking, to some extent, reflects my upbringing in childhood, which was built more from human contact than from playing with plastic toys.

Barbara and I both believed in the importance of human contact when it came to parenting. We wanted to spend more time with our children when they weren't in school. We were part of their lives by being present at school-related events and spending time with them at home while they were doing their homework. Barbara was devoted to this for many years.

Even though we understood early on that no parent can always protect their children from possible harm or racism in America, we also knew that we could assure them our availability if they needed us. We decided to do whatever it took to make our children happy and provide them with a good education and whatever else they might need. We decided to raise our children instead of focusing only on building our careers and creating wealth. Sometimes we both had to work at more than two jobs to make ends meet. We delayed vacations or trips; some years we simply skipped such trips. At that time, and going forward through their growing up days, our priority was meeting all the necessary needs of our children. We always had high expectations of ourselves as well as our sons. Aiming high and doing our best was the marching order. We both believed in church life and involvement in church communities wherever we lived.

Looking back, I don't think we could have gotten where we did if we hadn't come to an agreement on what is important in life beyond money. We trusted each other on everything, especially with money. We may have had disagreements and arguments on various issues, but never about money. I believe the issue of money was settled when we decided that we would have only one checking account, and that Barbara would pay our bills. This commitment was made soon after we were married. I don't remember paying bills by check because that was Barbara's role within our family. Recently, we decided to manage our banking through an online system, so now we both manage our account online.

Belize, Central America

As I hinted above, Barbara and I rented out our 14th street house and traveled to the country of Belize with our 18-month-old son. Two years earlier, Belize had gained its independence from Great Britain. It is a beautiful country bordered on the east by the Caribbean Sea, by Guatemala and Honduras to the west and south, and by Mexico to the north. The total population in Belize was 450,000 at that time. We stayed in Belize as Directors of the Study Service Term (SST) for 12 months. Each semester, 24 students from the college were sent to us.

The overall experience was very good for our family. However, the work was stressful. Shouldering a responsibility of this magnitude at such a young age was overwhelming. The responsibility was constantly on our minds.

The SST (or study abroad) programs are not easy to run. They involve great responsibility and the most challenging work one can experience. And yet, this work was also the most rewarding for us.

While on SST, we were not only the directors of the program, but also acted as friends, professors, counselors, dean of students, directors and more. After some 20 years, we still have some contact with a few of the students. It is simply a life-changing experience for both students and leaders. We enjoyed the people and the country in general. We enjoyed the seafood and also made a lot of good friends. In particular, we were good friends with Dr. Colvel Young, who was a regular speaker for our students. Dr. Young was later appointed as the Governor General of the country. We directed a successful program for a year, and then we returned to the States.

Major Family Event: My Parents' Visit

My parents came to visit us from Ethiopia for 5 months (November 1984-March 1985).

Back to Goshen for a Year

During the 1983-1984 academic year, I worked at Goshen College teaching and directing special programs. During this time I also finalized my decision to go to graduate school and work on my doctorate. Another very important event that I planned was organizing my parents' visit to the United States.

Organizing this visit was the most rewarding project I ever worked on with my brothers. Our parents came to the States for a visit for about five months. To our surprise, our parents were shocked mainly by a North American winter more than anything else they saw or experienced. Since we lived in different parts of the country, our parents traveled to see Teshome and Solomon, who were then living in New Mexico and Colorado. It was a very memorable experience, and included the most gratifying time we spent with our parents.

After our parents went back to Ethiopia, I was still serious about going through with my plan to further my education. This would involve visiting universities in order to check out graduate programs, and then interviewing for assistantships or fellowships that would allow me to support myself for the following three to four years. At the same time, we put our house on the market to sell and got ready to move so that I could go to graduate school.

Major Family Event: Ph.D. Program and Ashenafi

I enrolled in a Ph.D. program, and Barbara and I packed and moved to Carbondale, Illinois so I could attend Illinois University-Carbondale.

On December 10, 1984, Ashenafi was born in Carbondale.

Southern Illinois University

After visiting a number of campuses, I finally decided to attend Southern Illinois University in Carbondale. I was, of course, offered a good assistantship package for the first two years, and a fellowship for my third and final year while I was writing my dissertation. It was a good program and turned out to be a wonderful match for both me and my family.

This journey to graduate school for the second time was nothing short of an extraordinary experience for an ordinary person. My assistantship paid for all of my school tuition and fees. I had about a $350.00 stipend (pocket money) coming in every month. Even though this was a great help it was not enough to support a family of four. The equity money we got from the sale of our house in Goshen went straight to our savings account so we could earn monthly interest from a Certificate of Deposit, which was around 10% back then.

In order to have a comfortable life while in school, I took out a student loan. In three years, I racked up a $21,000 loan payable in ten years. I was grateful for the availability of the loan, and I did not miss one payment before I paid all of it off in ten years. Where else can this happen but in America?

About four months into my program, our second son, Ashenafi, was born on December 12, 1984. This was the day I was supposed to take an end of semester final exam. Ashenafi was born at 6:00 AM Monday morning. I took my final exam at 6:00 PM the evening of the same day.

The three year program went well, and so, as planned, I completed my Ph.D. in High Education Administration ahead of schedule. For both me and Barbara, the time we spent in grad school was the most rewarding time for our family. We spent plenty of time together as a family. We went to parks almost every weekend. Going to the children's library every weekend was another regular ritual for all three years when we lived at Southern. We developed a Friday evening regular schedule of going to the university fitness center. Overall, the Southern Illinois experience was the most positive and enriching experience we all had as a family. As busy as I was with my class work, it was important to me to have had carved out time to spend with my children while they were growing up.

Major Family Events

We purchased our first home computer (K-PRO II). In 1986, my mother died at age 75 from pneumonia.

Part IV: My Post-Ph.D. Life

The First Job After I Earned My Ph.D.

I graduated from Southern Illinois University on May 17, 1987. I had been applying and interviewing for my first job after I earned a terminal degree. I even had a couple of job offers with much better pay, but the locations would not have been a good place to raise children. I turned down opportunities until I found a better fit for me and my family. Then, I was offered a position at Manchester College in Northern Indiana as an Assistant Dean, Director of Minority Affairs, and Assistant Professor of Psychology. All three responsibilities made for a combined salary of only $22,000. Well, that was the market then and I wasn't about to complain. We purchased a house in Manchester, which we both liked. Our children were ready for school—Kaleab was ready for first grade and Ashenafi was ready for preschool.

I was happy to gain employment and moved my family to Northern Indiana. However, to make ends meet, I also signed up with Indiana University, at the Kokomo campus, to teach evening classes as an adjunct professor of psychology. I did that for five years until we moved to Goshen.

We lived in Manchester for five years, and then we felt it was time to move again. It was a small town with all of its accompanying challenges, and for the sake of our children, we decided to move to a bigger city. Around the same time, in 1990, I was offered a Dean of Students position at the University of Michigan-Flint, which I declined. About a year later, in 1991, I was contacted by Goshen College to take the position of the Director of a new Multicultural Education Program (the title soon changed to Vice President). I was also to serve as an Associate Professor of Psychology.

While in Manchester, Barbara liked the people, the town and the community in general more than I did, and the kids were doing fine in school, except for some social issues. Looking back, the move was the biggest and best decision we made at that time because of our children, believing that Goshen would offer better schools, a bigger city and more friends (even for Barbara and I to reconnect with our old friends in the community). So, overall, considering the alternatives, we felt it was an excellent fit for all of us.

One last thing about my experience at Manchester College was that, in 1991, I co-led a three-week travel and study program called "Cross Cultural Psychology" in the former Soviet Union and Eastern Europe. It involved 38 students.

Our Children

When we lived in Manchester, and then later on in Goshen, one of our goals was to do everything possible to see that our children went to the best school in the community we lived in. Of course, another goal was for them to go to a good college. I do not think we lamented the decisions we made, as they gave our children a good foundation for their education. Their education, of course, originally started at home (not homeschooling) with Barbara and all of the support we gave them. Even our movement from job to job was dictated by the concerns we had regarding educational opportunities and social issues that could potentially affect our children. We both had the opportunity for other jobs and more money, but the two things that made us choose these communities were the availability of good educational systems and the opportunity to spend more time with our children. It was clear to us, even back then, that we'd never be able to go back and undo anything. So, instead of focusing on money, we made our children our top priority. Barbara stayed at home until our youngest child finished middle school.

Major Family Event: My Return to Ethiopia

In June of 1991, after 11 years in the United States, I returned to Ethiopia to visit family. As noted previously, I came to the U.S. in 1972 and had not been back since. Ethiopia was my country, and so I missed my people, my friends, the culture, the food, the music and everything else about the place. Ethiopia was where I belonged.

Soon, I realized that time was slipping away. I was missing my family terribly, even to the point that I was almost forgetting the faces of my relatives in Ethiopia. This part of my journey is recorded in the DVD titled "Greetings from relatives-Visit to Ethiopia." The video tells the story of my family, with my journey embedded into the narrative.

Back to Goshen (Again)

When we moved again, we decided to stay put until our children had finished high school and gone off to college. So, when we moved back to Goshen, we stayed for 12 years, and spent 10 years in the same house. We loved our house on Eighth Street, and we loved our neighbors to the left. However, the neighbors to our right were disrespectful, uncultured, and bad-mannered. All of this is to say that they were less than desirable. We managed to live with neighbors we did not like because our focus was on our children. The school system was good and we did not want to move again. This was the long-term commitment we made toward our children's education.

Our children did well in the public school system. They were both highly involved in sports, music and leadership activities. They were also equally active in the church MYF program. Our sons played almost every sport available in their school: soccer, basketball, football, swimming, baseball, track, and tennis. They were even in the marching band. This means we had to attend all of their sporting events. We drove to every small town in Elkhart County and beyond. We also followed them to traveling sports events, whether they were on weekdays or weekends. We always made time for them.

The rule in our house was that we would pay for any school-related activities. Also, we always celebrated report card days by eating out, no matter what grades they'd received (though they mostly received good grades).

We believe our sons learned a lot about their place in the community, who they are, and what their limitations were, by using good judgment sometimes, and through trial and error at other times, as is the case with most adolescence. I would like to believe that Barbara and I, along with our children, early on in our journey, together we learned that social entrance is not all fun and game all the time, especially in communities we choose to live in.

I can say that because of our children, our world has been enlarged and has also become more interesting to live in. They made good choices and decisions and did well for themselves overall. Because of where they are and what they chose to do, we became hopeful about our world.

As a father, I can say our children turned out to be nothing short of our dream. We never experienced any problems beyond the expected parent-adolescent conflicts over curfew or school work. Of course, we also displayed the tough love that's ascribed to good parents. Sometimes we struggled with this, and sometimes it did not feel good in the moment, but, looking back, it did pay off. Now, we rejoice at the outcome. Today, given where our children are in their own journeys, we are grateful for the information we were able to provide them, and for the decisions our children made. They set out to chase their own dreams, they are managing themselves well and we are very proud of our sons. Looking back, our sons made their own decisions based on the information they were given. While we were still in Goshen, Barbara also went back to college to earn another degree. This time, it was a teaching degree from Goshen College. She taught in Elkhart for several years before we moved to California.

Major Family Event: Family Trip to Ethiopia

In June and July of 1998, our family (the four of us) traveled to Ethiopia for a month-long vacation. This was the first visit for the boys and Barbara.

Family Trip

Barbara and I felt that traveling as a family to my birthplace of Ethiopia to meet my relatives for the first time was one of the most important things we did for our family. The trip was expensive, and we did not have much in our savings, but we decided to borrow money so that we could travel with our children and try to connect them to their heritages – Ethiopia.

We felt that they had to have some sense of connectedness and roots in the country I came from. Toward that end, we both believed that every penny we borrowed was a good investment.

On our way to Ethiopia, we had a 10-hour layover in London. We decided to take the tube (subway) from the airport to visit downtown London. That, too, was a good and worthwhile experience.

While in Ethiopia, we flew from Addis Ababa to Dire Dawa to visit my brother Sisay's family. We then rented a car to take us to my hometown of Deder. We also traveled to Harar to visit Gedamu's family, and then to the historic city of Hara. Then, back to Addis Ababa so we could make another trip to the north. In the north, we traveled to the city of Baher Dar. We flew from Addis to Baher Dar, and then we rented a boat to visit the ancient churches on the island in Lake Tana. As some of my readers know, that is where the famous Nile River begins and the only river I know that travels north until it reaches Egypt. From there, we hired a guide to take us to the famous and magnificent Nile River Fall.

Everywhere we went in Ethiopia we were greeted and welcomed by everyone. My Ethiopian family members, in particular, were so happy to meet Barbara and our children. The joyous welcoming celebration was unbelievable (watch the family visit to Ethiopia video). Some of my friends invited us to their homes, and this also made the visit very enjoyable. Our visit to Ethiopia was concluded by shopping at the well-known Merkato in Addis, and also in an open market in Taiwan when we were in Dire Dawa. Looking back now, we wish we had done more of these trips together as a family before our children settled down in their professions.

My Profession

What did I do for a living, and how did I support a family? After I finished graduate school, from the mid-80's to the early 2000's, I was in the prime of my profession. As I stated in one of the previous sections, in all my adult professional life, I served as a professor and university administrator. I did a lot of consulting on the side, both locally and nationally. I was involved in diversity training, and a new anti-racism training program affiliated with the Mennonite Central Committee (MCC). I developed a new course, Analysis of Racism and Power, which I taught for six years. I was active in the community, mainly educating the public in the area of diversity and race relations. I developed an interest in the area of demography and started sharing my research about the demographic shift taking place in the United States.

Sometimes, my team and I were well-received and invited to share our findings with strong interest. There were also some people who did not believe what we were reporting. People were suspicious and did not want to believe that this country would lose its dominant white culture at some point in the future. Even when scholars repeatedly published evidence of demographic change in the country—change that we needed to accommodate—most people decided to deny rather than to help plan and be prepared for the future. Franklin D. Roosevelt once said:

"We cannot prepare the future for our children, but we can prepare our children for the future."

Others simply brushed it off and dismissed the facts, until the mid-1990's, when the Hispanic populations started taking over Midwest cities, including some in Illinois and Indiana. Normally, the Hispanic populations were more pronounced in some southern, eastern, and western states, but not in the Midwestern states such as Illinois, Indiana, Missouri and Ohio. In 2013, a published study, which was aired all over the network news, showed that for the first time ever, America was populated with 50.4 percent persons of color. The projection was that, in the near future, there would be no single majority ethnic group in the United States.

Occupation-Related Travel

My occupation provided me with travel opportunities. I traveled professionally and with family. I was fortunate to have had the opportunity to travel, both nationally and internationally. One highlight of my professional travel was when I was selected to participate in the Fulbright program, which allowed me to spend six weeks in Germany so I could learn about their higher education system.

There's one other noteworthy job-related travel experience: I proposed, developed and directed a new SST program in Ethiopia from 2001 to 2002, while I was still at Goshen College. I met quite a few famous people in Ethiopia during this time, such as Afework Tekle and Haile Gebrselassie.

Haile Gebrselassie is a retired Ethiopian long-distance track and road-running athlete. He won two Olympic gold medals over 10,000 meters and four World Championship titles in the event. He won the Berlin Marathon four times consecutively and also had three straight wins at the Dubai Marathon. Furthermore, he won four world titles indoors and was the 2001 World Half Marathon Champion.

Afework Tekle was the most honorable Maître Artist World Laureate and was one of Ethiopia's most celebrated artists. He was particularly known for his paintings on African and Christian themes, as well as for his stained glass.

Study Service Term (SST) in Ethiopia

While leading the SST program in Ethiopia, I kept a journal. The excerpts below are entries from that journal.

Entry from November 30, 2001:

Tuesday was my last day at Goshen College before heading to Ethiopia. Kaleab is in his third year of college and living in the residence hall. Just before I left Goshen he called me and asked if we could visit over coffee at the college snack shop. As we sat down to have coffee and started talking, I just couldn't talk and my emotions took over. Kaleab quickly noted that I was getting emotional and he tried to be strong, or at least, he tried to hide his emotions while at the same time comforting me. He tried to distract me by asking me questions.

We talked for a while and we said goodbye to each other, and I could tell it was hard for both of us. As I hugged him and said bye, we both started crying and Kaleab said, "Dad, I will miss you because you will be gone for 5 months." We both tried to comfort one another and I am sure he was troubled about it, too. I told him I would stay in touch. I even invited him to go with his mother to the South Bend airport, him to go with his mother to the South Bend airport, where she was planning on dropping me off, but it did not work out for him to go. After we departed, I called Kaleab from South Bend, from Chicago, and finally from Washington, D.C., just before I left for Ethiopia. I never felt so connected to my family as I did on that day.

I was close to wrapping up the orientation part of the Addis Ababa program when this incident occurred: on January 30, 2002, one of my students was injured by a motorcycle rider while she was crossing the street. That took a lot of emotional energy out of me and my students. The injured student had to fly back to California, where her parents lived, for treatment. Luckily, she recovered well. She actually came back to Ethiopia to join the rest of the group about a couple of weeks before we wrapped up the program.

Entry from April 3, 2002:

A bad day to remember—it was around 9:20 AM when I found out my car had been broken into in front of the commercial bank where I did my banking. While I was in the bank, my car was parked out in front, and someone stole my computer. When I walked back to my car, I found the car broken into. My computer was missing, as were a bag with a digital camera and many other important records. For the moment I couldn't believe what happened, and I only felt helpless and hopeless. I was confused and panicked and did not know what to do. I asked people standing around if they can help me or if they'd seen the person who took the items from the car. No one would help. It was a very difficult moment for me. Never felt so lonely and empty. In about an hour I went to a computer shop and sent out an email to the SST office in Goshen and to my wife, Barbara. A lot of friends and neighbors came to help, but my computer and all the items in the bag were nowhere to be found. I went to the main branch of the bank and closed my bank account and stopped any payments from that day on.

I felt so low in energy. I did not have any idea what to do and where to begin. I lost so many documents, and with the computer I lost everything I'd worked on and documented for the past 4 months. There was not much I could do at this point. It was about 10:00 PM and I was not sure if I could sleep that night.

I said to myself, I know this did not happen out of neglect, or carelessness, but as an act of violation against my rights. There wasn't much I could do. I said to myself, I have to put myself together by tomorrow morning. I had too much to do and my students were about to return from their service locations to Addis Ababa for debriefing and to report on their experiences. It was now out of my control, and as difficult as it was, it was time to move on.

Major Family Event

My father died at age 98 in June of 2002.

A Move to the West Coast

After 12 years in the same community, and after our sons finished public school, we decided to move again. This time, the move would be to California. All of my moves from one institution to another were driven by better professional opportunities, better compassion and better financial resources for the family.

By the time Ashenafi finished high school and enrolled at Goshen College, Kaleab had graduated from college and accepted a job as a math teacher at Goshen High School. Barbara and I decided to move to California. We moved near Fresno Pacific University, where I was hired by the university to be the Chief of Student Affairs Officer and Dean of Students. I was also a member of the teaching faculty and taught a course each semester. Barbara decided to no longer teach and joined the corporate world. She was hired as the operations manager of a cookie company. Barbara was happy with her job, and I also loved what I was doing, so we both immensely enjoyed our new home in Fresno, California.

I think California was, and still is, the place to be. The weather was always nice, the mountains were close, the parks were immaculate and the drive from our home to the ocean only took a couple of hours. Most important for us was that we enjoyed the farmer's market year round. We were able to purchase fresh produce every week, and very cheaply.

We enjoyed Fresno, and it was one of our most wonderful experiences in comparison to the other places where we lived. We had a lot of visitors and we enjoyed hosting people in our house. The house had 4 bedrooms and 3 full bathrooms and a swimming pool in the backyard.

In Fresno, one activity we both enjoyed (as you might guess) was going to the open farmer's market. We never missed the Saturday market unless we were out of town. The other enjoyable and memorable activity was going to the national parks in the surrounding areas. Since we did not invest in any kind of community involvement, we made time to travel and see around California.

Our California experience was hampered by one major problem: we were far away from our children and other family members. Since we were three time zones away, even a flight from the West Coast to the Midwest took an entire day. During our second year in California, Kaleab and Alyssa got married and moved to Pittsburgh, PA, where both of them were attending graduate school. Barbara and I thought that if we could find employment in the Midwest or on the East Coast, we would consider moving closer to our children. So, I started looking for job opportunities in the Midwest.

During Thanksgiving of 2007, just before we moved back to the Midwest, Tadelech and Solomon came to visit us in Fresno. The plan was for Teshome and Gedamu to also join as at the same time. Gedamu was visiting the States and staying with Tamene in Colorado. However, since Gedamu left for Ethiopia early, Teshome also decided not to come at that time.

Move to Wisconsin

After almost six years in California, I was offered a position in Fond du Lac, Wisconsin, at a Catholic University (Marion University) to serve as the Founding Vice President of Equity and Inclusion and as an associate professor of psychology. I took the position and moved there. Barbara joined me three months later. She was also hired by Marion University.

Although it was a good position and the package was excellent, and although the position allowed us to move closer to family and friends, this position did not last long. I enjoyed working with the president of the university, as she and I got along well, but I was not sure whether the president trusted her management team, with whom I worked. Since most members of her management team were recent hires, the team was in the process of being built. Unlike most university president I worked with, she was most interested in improving the campus culture and diversity. Her relationships with the provost, some administrators, and board members were noticeably wobbly, to say the least. In many ways, for me, this was a dream job, and I wish I had stayed there until my retirement. However, while it lasted, it was good. I have no regrets for accepting that position at Marion University.

The university was in a deep hole financially. The weekly executive meetings were usually not pleasant.

In March of 2009, the board had an emergency meeting to ask the president to resign and vacate her office in less than a week. This turned out to be a disaster for all the people she hired. The Board

Chair became the new interim president and cleaned house by eliminating 25 positions for faculty and staff, including three vice presidents who had been hired by the president. I was one of these three vice presidents.

About two months before the president was asked to leave, before we even knew anything about the university's financial problems, Barbara and I visited Indianapolis at the invitation of Ashenafi, in order to look for a house for the future. Since we'd decided not to purchase a home in Wisconsin, choosing instead to rent, we wanted to invest in a home where we could maybe retire in the future. We found a house we liked, so we went ahead and purchased it in January of 2009.

This has to have been one of the biggest decisions we've made within the past ten years. The square footage of the house was adequate, the floor plan was perfect, as if it had been built just for us, and most of all, the price was right. We also couldn't have found a better location.

It was ironic that we purchased our new house in Indy two months before we had any idea what was going to happen at Marion University. Both of our positions at the university were eliminated, so we moved to our new home in Indianapolis.

For many reasons, the move to our new home in July of 2009 worked out well. We enjoyed living in the vibrant city of Indianapolis. Perhaps this served as a good speed bump in our life together.

After moving to our new home, Barbara and I both decided to give ourselves a 6-month sabbatical. We decided to take it easy and look for other possibilities in the area. Since this was during the middle of the economic crisis in America, finding jobs in our profession was almost impossible.

Major Historical Event: The First African American President

Back in 2008, before our move to Indianapolis, I was invited by a local newspaper (the REPORTER) to write an opinion piece ahead of the election, assuming Senator Barack Obama would win. This is what I wrote two nights before the election. It was published on Wednesday morning, November 25, 2008:

> *"This election is the most anticipated and the most historic not only here but around the world. As an Ethiopian American, I am delighted to be part of this incredible moment of history in America. This is the third time I have voted. I voted in the past with excitement, hope and admiration of the candidate of my choice. This time however, I even voted early because I see this as a vote for hope and new direction. The two candidates gave us many good ideas to think about before we cast our votes.*
>
> *Obama's opponent was unable to communicate his vision for the nation. He simply left us with the assumption that things will stay the same – a governing philosophy, as has been for years past, where the poor will get poorer and the rich will get richer and our country will remain divided.*

On the other hand, a forward thinking Obama offered the possibility of new direction for economic development, education, healthcare and most of all, hope to unite this racially divided country.

I am convinced and very hopeful that with President Obama in the White House, I can see the United States' stature around the world being revived to where it was a couple of decades ago. We were then highly respected and looked to by many nations for leadership.

Listening to his speeches, his manner and communication skills, Obama's ability to organize all people from all walks of life, convinced me to believe that he will lead America to better social and economic conditions than where we are today. Obama has the ability to galvanize leaders of the world to improve the global economy. Economic and diplomatic relationships with other nations will improve under the Obama leadership to create global peace and prosperity.

I am convinced that the psychology of relationships not only for us here as brothers and sisters, but worldwide, will see a psyche transformation.

I am hopeful that because of President Obama, a new level of understanding will emerge of how we interact with one another. By doing so, Hispanics, Asian-Americans and Native Americans will not feel that Obama will only affect the black-white

> *relationships. Finally, I am convinced that Obama has done his part; now it is up to us to follow our leader to a better day ahead."*

My Political Opinion of President Obama -- 2015

By 2013, the challenges were mounting. Unemployment was at a high of 7.3% and over 15 million people were unemployed. The deficit was at an all-time high and experts told the public that the deficit would cost every American $43,000 in today's money.

It's important to remember, however, that President Obama was doing what needed to be done: he reformed health care, pulled troops out of Iraq, reformed the financial institution, and extended the unemployment benefits to the unemployed. The right wing Republicans were going out of their minds. The new Tea Party was growing in numbers; Republicans and the Tea Party group wanted President Obama to fail. I wondered what it would be like ten years from now.

By 2014, six years into his two-term presidency, President Obama had done all the right things for the country. His policy brought economic recovery, improvement in unemployment, and new health care to help over 30 million uninsured Americans. However, it seems like President Obama was the most hated person by the Republican Congress and other whites in America.

The white's systemic and individual racism in America had just come out of the woods. Lawmakers in the House, the Senate, and all over the United States, including in state governments, clearly showed their true colors. Racism showed up in the most ugly and vivid form: denying the President the authority to pass policies that would help the middle class. Police from California to New York and everywhere in between started targeting and killing black youth in particular.

Additionally, it became obvious that whites did not want President Obama to make additional history, and that they wanted his legacy to be limited, so that he was remembered only as the first black President. President Obama happened to be very smart and slick in how he handled these lawmakers. No matter how much they wanted to undermine him, he will be remembered as a President who saved, not only the American economy, but also the world economy from major collapse (depression). He came up with health care for all Americans. He initiated a two-year tuition-free college program. Because of his policy, unemployment dropped from over 10%, when he took office, to 5%. He ended the war in Iraq and reduced the number of troops in Afghanistan.

During this presidency, the policy he implemented against the Republican policymakers saved the country from going into a depression. The health care law was passed, a historic immigration policy was crafted, unemployment improved and people went back to work, gas prices dropped to a five year low, and the economy turned around. The stock market is at a historic high at 19,000 points.

In 2015, the Republicans continued to hate the President so much that they were trying to run foreign policy. Six years after the law on health care was signed, they still tried to undo it, though they had no plan just from my reading and watching I get the impression that President Obama. President Obama was the most hated person by some white people in my lifetime. They were trying to deny him a good legacy, but he was one of the smartest presidents.

During President Obama's administration, when interest rates were at an all-time low, the unemployment rate was below six percent by September 2015, and the stock market was enjoying a historical record of 17,000 points. Throughout President Obama's administration, despite the great things he accomplished, about one-third of all Americans still disliked him because of his skin color. It sounds, and feels like, we are back in the 1970's, when whites had very little respect for people of color. The social dilemma which the country experienced in the 70's is, unfortunately, persisting today.

After these many years of observing the social and political complexities in this country, I've concluded that living under the umbrella of the system of white supremacy in America is nothing but hell on earth for people of color. It stings and pains and it has the capacity to destroy a person's confidence and self-esteem.

Major Family Events of the Past Decade (the 2000s)

1) Barbara's father died in Memphis, TN

2) Our sons graduated from college

3) Kaleab and Alyssa got married on Jul 24, 2004

4) Ashenafi had some wonderful performances

5) Both of our sons became employed

6) Both Kaleab and Alyssa earned Master's degrees

7) Kaleab completed his Ph.D. (the first of
the second generation of our family)

8) Helen and Sisay got married in
Amsterdam—I traveled to Europe for the
wedding along with Barbara and Surafel

2010 and Beyond

Six months into our new life in Indianapolis, things were going well. After 30 some years of working hard, we enjoyed our time off from work. One thing that happened during 2010 was the birth of Hannah, our new granddaughter. She was the most beautiful baby I'd ever seen, although I said the same thing when my sons were born. We hope to see Hannah as often as possible.

Both Barbara and I started looking for jobs in our area, but as stated earlier, this was difficult due to the country's economic crisis. Things in higher education were only getting worse. After a while, I even contemplated early retirement, but I found out I wouldn't be eligible for any government benefits. I launched my own consulting business, but marketing was a challenge. Barbara took a part-time position at a department store called Macy's, and I kept looking for work in my field.

Just to comment on how bad the job market was in this country, in a year and a half alone, I sent out over 120 applications, in 28 states, and in four different countries. I had a number of Skype interviews and campus interviews, and yet none of them materialized. Just to stay busy, I looked for a job even at Lowes, Home Depot, and Meijer stores, and yet none of them would hire me because I was over-educated (overqualified) for their positions. Finally, I consulted with a friend and he told me to do away with any mention of my Ph.D. and the formal résumé and to just pretend to be uneducated. Using his advice, I was hired at Meijer, part-time in the systems division. At the same time, I joined a consulting, executive search firm, Archer-Martin, as a Principal Associate.

During that year, I enjoyed doing yard work and writing. Our yard was always well-kept and looked immaculate. This brought me joy. Both Barbara and I seemed to enjoy spending time outdoors planting flowers and trimming shrubs just for fun. I also spent hours at a time in front of my computer just writing and developing ideas. I produced a 28-page small handbook for Meserete Kirsitos (MK) College. Teshome and I were in the process of developing an idea to create the "Abebe and Associate Consulting Firm." I was also asked to expand and re-do the MK College handbook to make it more generic so it could be used widely in Ethiopia.

One other important thing to note is the proximity of Indianapolis to the locations of our other family members. As stated earlier, Barbara and I wanted to be closer to our family members, so that we were at least within driving distance from most of them. When we moved to Indianapolis, I think we accomplished this in regards to most family members: Teshome lived only 2 hours west of us in Illinois, as did Asegedech; Solomon and his family lived in Indianapolis, as did Lidet and her family; Ashenafi lived only about 10 miles away from us; and Kaleab and Alyssa lived in Pittsburgh, PA, which was about a 6-hour drive by car to the east. Of course, Shawle and Mary Jane lived about 10 hours away, Tamene and his family lived out in Colorado, and Surafel and Jessica lived with their children about 12 hours away in Minnesota.

Major Family Events in 2010

1) Emanuel Assefa was born in January of 2010

2) Barbara and I became grandparents—
Hannah was born on February 20, 2010

3) In June of 2010 our house was hit by lightning,
causing a hole in the roof, but no one was hurt

4) Nitsuh got married on August 7, 2010

Mismake's Unexpected Journey to the States

I decided to include Mismake's short story here because she is very significant to our family history. She and Tadelech are the only two daughters among six brothers. Mismake, unlike the rest of us, has impacted the life of every single person in our family. She took care of mom and dad in their old age while we were absent from the country chasing the good life in America. She was always there for every one of our family members when they needed her.

She has gone well beyond the call of duty, and always without complaining or asking for help from any of us. She was there for Gedamu and his family, she was with Tadelech during her daughter, Kelemua's, tragic death, she was there for Sisay and his family, etc. The list goes on. Without Mismake, Tadelech's wonderful new house would not have been built. I would not have even dared to start the Study Abroad Program (SST) in Ethiopia for Goshen College if it had not been for Mismake. She's simply been a sister who never complained or asked for anything, a sister who was always gentle, calm, helpful and loving. We are indeed blessed with a sister who is full of grace and dignity.

The following is a timeline of Mismake's unexpected journey to America, which she embarked upon for medical reasons:

-On August 10, 2010, we received a call from Ethiopia informing us that Mismake was not feeling well and was planning to come to the U.S. for treatment.

-On August 21, 2010, Mismake Abebe arrived in Indianapolis, IN. She was admitted to the Simon Cancer Center in Indianapolis. A series of blood tests revealed what none of us expected: Acute Leukemia. Mismake was discharged from the hospital on September 16, in order to continue her treatment as an out-patient for the next 6-8 months.

-On February 4, 2011, Ledet and Million, and their children moved to New Jersey. Mismake and Girma decided to stay in Ledet's apartment for the next 3-4 months until she was finished with her treatment. Unlike what Mismake did for her parents, her own daughter did not have the same compassion to take care of her own mother, when she left her in an unfurnished apartment with no bed for her mother to sleep on. Of course, as I have heard many say people say, this is the American way and children are not socialized to care about their parents. I know for sure, this is not an Ethiopian way. Some of us decided to support our sister and her husband by paying their monthly rent and meeting other needs for the next 3 months.

-On October 7, Sisay came from Holland to see Mismake. He planned to stay in Indianapolis for about 10 days. Sisay was so disappointed about Mismake's living conditions and where she lived that he made his contribution by cleaning the apartment and painting the rooms to make the place nice and comfortable.

Back to My Journey

In Indianapolis, I was not sure what was next for me in terms of retirement or regular work. For the next 4 years, until I reached retirement age, I decided to keep doing what I was doing and enjoy my time writing and reading, which were less stressful than regular work. Previously, I had not had the chance to do such a thing in my adult life. All I knew was work, more work, and nothing else. Now that our children were grown up and gone, Barbara and I both had more time to do what we wanted, such as traveling to visit friends and family members.

Since I had to wait four more years before retiring, in the meantime I decided to look for wisdom based on my past experiences. As for the future, I would look for more opportunities to make a difference for those who were less fortunate than I, and for those in need both in my community and in the larger world. I could not foresee what was to come.

At the end of 2010, in terms of new job opportunities, not much was happening. Our unemployment insurance that we'd paid into for over 28 years had run out after 15 months. As reported over and over again, at that point there were over 15 million people nationwide who had been unemployed for more than two years. The overall economic situation of the country was predicted to be grim in the foreseeable future. The Obama administration was in limbo. His own party members were almost deserting him, and his ability to govern came into question as Republicans took over the House of Representatives in the November, 2010 election. As many things were in question and uncertainty loomed over us, we waited for the unexpected, rejoiced for what we had in the present, prayed for good health, and hoped for the best.

In November, 2010, I went ahead and applied for the Social Security early retirement program, since I would be turning 62 in January. I was not sure if I was going to follow through, but I saw it as an option if full employment was not possible within the next two or three months. In January, I decided not to go through with early retirement, so, Social Security was put on hold.

Back To Work (February, 2011)

As described above, Barbara and I went without meaningful full-time employment for two years. In the process, we were depleting our life savings. We both had part-time jobs without benefits, and they didn't bring in much income. Even this part-time work, however, helped us get out of the house. It felt good to go to work in the morning.

Earlier, I explained that I found a part-time work at Meijer. Let me describe that in more detail here:

My part-time job was not considered glamorous. I thought the small earnings would help with gas and spending money while I am still looking to get back to higher education. The store manager at Meijer was very reluctant to hire me after he'd heard my story. He asked me if I really wanted to work with these uneducated people. I told him I didn't mind working there until I found something else. I ended up working there for about a year.

I made $7.50 an hour. I wanted to mention this for a couple of reasons: first, to emphasize that I gained an understanding of how the retail world functions; second, to show that I simply didn't want to sit around all day doing nothing, so I wanted to do something for at least half of the day; and third, just to make a comparison with the previous job I had, which paid me in a six figures, annual salary. This was an unforgettable and valuable experience that enabled me to see how people struggle to make a living. It was very hard for me to understand how so many people who work at retail stores, like Meijer or Wal-mart, can earn only $7-10 an hour and yet manage to support themselves and their families. It made me think about what I did for a living, the time and money I invested in my education, and what I had and how grateful I should be for the kind of work I did and the kind of life I lived.

I also learned how management and employees interact. I learned about the culture of mistrust and control. The focus of management was always about production and profit-making, not so much about respect for employees. Since this was during a bad recession in the country, there was a widely understood perception among management that if one employee left, another one was waiting to come in the door. Even the clock-in and clock-out machine would not let you check in to work if you were five minutes late, and you couldn't leave five minutes early. All this was foreign to me since I'd previously been in a university setting and had never had to report my comings and goings at work.

One year later, in mid-January, I received a call inviting me to an interview at the MCC Great Lakes office for the Executive Director position. I had applied for this position on December 14, 2010. My first interview was on Monday night, February 7. Three days later I was invited back for a second interview for Monday, February 14. On Tuesday, February 15, I received a call from the chair of the search committee, and who was also serving as the chair of the board of directors at that time, offering me the position. Two days later, I sent an email accepting the offer.

The following is a heading of the news release from February 25, 2011, describing my new employment with MCC:

MENNONITE CENTRAL COMMITTEE (MCC) GREAT LAKES NEWS RELEASE

Blurb: *Zenebe Abebe will draw from a wealth of experiences as he becomes MCC Great Lakes Executive Director.*

Zenebe Abebe named MCC Great Lakes executive director

    =====================//=======================

I was excited that the Mennonite Central Committee (MCC) Great Lakes Board of Directors has named me as the organization's CEO or Executive Director. At the time of the appointment, I was living in Indianapolis. I was told that my responsibility will be planning for and managing Great Lakes staff and program, representing MCC to the Great Lakes constituency, overseeing fundraising and collaborating within the MCC system. I was excited about working closely with five other regional executive directors to provide overall leadership for MCC's in the U.S.

By this time, I had worked for Mennonite, and Mennonite-related, educational institutions for nearly 30 years in management, program development and teaching. I believe my connections with the Anabaptist community, both regionally and globally, will be an asset to the MCC system.

Because of my past 30 years professional work experience in Mennonite institutions, my core values are in concert with the core values of MCC Great Lakes and that is a major attraction for me. I believe that social justice for all and awareness of issues that inflict pain and suffering to others must be a top priority of all church-related institutions.

At this time, I was principal owner of an educational consulting, training and development firm in Indianapolis. At the time I was also principal associate of the Archer~Martin Executive Search Firm. Prior to that, I served as a vice president for equity and inclusion, and as a faculty member at Marion University, a liberal arts institution of higher education in Fond du Lac, Wisconsin. I accepted this position believing that I have transferable management skills from my earlier experiences, including almost six years at Fresno (Calif.) Pacific University as chief student affairs officer and professor of psychology, and 18 years at Goshen (Ind.) College, and most recently as a vice president for Multicultural Education.

Most importantly, I felt good about what I could bring to this responsibility, such as experience gained through extensive traveling and the ability to speak several languages. I developed a study abroad program in Ethiopia, my home country. I also led student groups in the former Soviet Union, Eastern Europe and Belize. Through the years, I stayed connected to a Mennonite church and at that time Barbara and I were attending Shalom Mennonite Church in Indianapolis.

This work will be quite a shift from what I have done for over 30 years in higher education. Since it mainly has to do with management, I feel good about the position, the people are different, expectations will be different and the way things are carried out will be very different. For the most part, I will have transferable sets of skills that would be helpful for a while.

Mennonite Central Committee Great Lakes

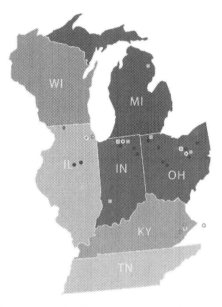

I was hired as an executive director to oversee the work of MCC Great Lakes, including the 7 states in this region, and to be responsible for the funds to be raised for the program.

Here's a little more information about Mennonite Central Committee (MCC): MCC in the U.S. is divided by four regions. There are four executive regional directors and one national executive director. A similar structure exists for Canada's MCC, where provincial executive directors serve as the CEOs of their respective provinces.

The MCC of the Great Lakes region is managed by 12 board members. I served the board as the CEO of the organization. My staff and I were responsible for 7 states, 389 congregations, 13 thrift shops (mainly in 3 states),

7 relief sales a year, and 8 meat canning sites. We were expected to raise $5-6 million annually. The MCC mission is simple: disaster relief, community development and peace and justice for all in the name of Christ.

I had never seen or experienced, or even heard of, an organization that was considered to be one of the most beloved church institutions in Mennonite circles. People and congregations give to MCC simply because they believe in what the organization is doing. Monetary donations and materials are given without asking for proof, so everything is based on trust. I personally enjoyed this experience because of the trust people had in the institution and my own understanding of this type of work. There was no competition. Instead, there is only collaboration to help those in need around the world. I started my new responsibility (calling) on Thursday, March 31, 2011 in Goshen, Indiana, and the following Monday night, April 4, 2011 my sister Mismake died in Indianapolis.

Mismake's Death

An unexpected event, for which none of us were prepared, took place in our family in 2011. Our beloved sister Mismake Abebe passed away at age 57 on Monday night, April 4th, after 8 months of cancer (Acute Leukemia) treatment in Indianapolis. Since the treatment was not working and the cancer was getting worse, Mismake decided to go home. She was supposed to fly out of Washington, D.C. on April 2, to go to her home in Ethiopia and wait for God's will. This did not happen because she died sooner. Her body was sent to Ethiopia on April 9, 2011 and she was buried in Addis Ababa. Her husband, daughter and son and our youngest sibling, Tamene, also flew to Ethiopia, on April 9, in order to be with the rest of our family in Addis Ababa.

Our older sister, Tadelech, who had just arrived on April 2, to be with Mismake, returned to Ethiopia on Thursday, April 7, to join the rest of the family. Tadelech visited with her baby sister for only two hours before Mismake was taken to the emergency room and lost consciousness. This was a very hard and unbearable experience for all my brothers and other family members. We rejoice in Mismake's good and productive life. She was the pillar of our family, the planner and the caretaker of our family in Ethiopia. She left us too soon and we will miss her forever.

This was the first real calamity in our family since Kelemua's death, and none of us were prepared for it. Mismake was the first sibling of eight to die. The age range of my brothers and sisters is spread out from the mid-50's to the mid-70's, and Mismake was the third youngest among these siblings. Suddenly, we had to somehow understand that death is part of the package.

We couldn't find an answer as to why our sister died so young, however for now, we can only simply wonder who would be next among the living and when. For now, though the situation is difficult, we will try to rejoice the life Mismake lived and the blessings she left us with. She left us with a legacy of greatness. She was gracious, dignified, and respectful of every human being who crossed her path. I can say that Mismake was very courageous. As she told me again and again, she was not afraid to die.

Three weeks after Mismake's death, the grief remained and I had to figure out how to deal with it. Someone told me a metaphor explaining grief as an ocean that comes at you in waves. At times, an ocean wave can come at you strong, forceful enough to sweep you off the beach. Other times it can even be strong enough to sweep you back to the ocean. Still other times, a gentle ocean wave comes at you, touches your feet, and goes right back. That is exactly what my experience was like in those first 3 weeks following Mismake's death.

Going Back to Ethiopia

By the end of October, I'd been working with MCC for over 6 months. All was well and I was traveling more than I thought I would. I would stay in Goshen four days a week, then travel in Indiana, Ohio, Illinois, Kentucky, Tennessee and West Virginia. This travel was more than I expected. My travels to other regions, and to Canada, were also unexpected. I usually spoke in churches one Sunday a month. I liked what I did, but I really didn't want to go away from my home every weekend. There was a lot to be done around the house, and Barbara usually worked on weekends, so the yard work was always waiting for me. At that time, this is simply what we had to work with.

During this time, Teshome and I planned to go to Ethiopia in December of 2011, to visit Gedamu, Tadelech, and other relatives. Teshome and I set our departure date for Saturday, December 17, 2011. This was going to be a fun trip, and yet at the same time it would be hard because Mismake would not be around for the first time. This was also going to be the first time for me and Teshome to be back in Ethiopia together in almost 40 years. We had each been home separately, but not at the same time. For the first time in almost 40 years, the four oldest siblings would be together again.

We returned from our Ethiopian trip on January 1, 2012. Did we have fun? Well, it was a wonderful time with family and friends. However, the impact of Mismake's death on both Gedamu and Tadelech was noticeable. They spoke about her loss and what life meant without Mismake.

More about MCC

After almost four years at my Mennonite Central Committee (MCC) responsibility, I made a number of observations. First, the MCC organization was too large and complex. There were about 1,000-1,100 volunteers and paid workers at any given time, and they were spread out in 60 different countries around the globe.

My responsibility for the Great Lakes region was to be sure that there was enough financial support for all of the volunteers, paid workers and other support staff. As I stated earlier, my region alone was expected to raise over $5-8 million annually in order to meet our international commitment to the overall MCC global programs. Amazingly, thanks to the support of constituencies, we always met, and even exceeded, our goals each of the five years I was with MCC.

Overall, I did find MCC to be a good place to work. For me, it was a wonderful fit in terms of management, responsibility, knowledge of people in the church, and familiarity with the culture. The churches' support of this organization is amazing. The board members I worked for were trusting and empowered me. I worked with some of the finest board chairs. Sometimes I found myself wishing I had worked many more years for MCC.

This was one place I worked where there was no competition. As a person coming in from another language, culture and from outside MCC experience, I always worked harder and did my job well. When I retire soon, MCC Great Leaks will be in its best financial position it has ever been. The supporters are so trusting of the organization and the staff. I had fine people to work with and they were all committed, and good at what they did. I never got tired and I always looked forward to doing whatever needed to be done. I traveled thousands of miles to do my work and yet, I was always excited to do it again the next morning. For me, this was the best professional experience I had. I am grateful for the opportunity I received to work for Mennonite Central Committee (MCC) in the U.S.

As I mentioned above, MCC is the most complex not-for-profit organization I have ever known, but it works. I'm sure the organization, great as it is, will continue to exist. However, MCC as a worldwide ministry of Anabaptist churches, sharing God's love and compassion to all in the name of Christ, will need to examine its workplace environment and its hiring practices. As respected as MCC is around the globe, it has some major imperfections that need to be addressed. Among others, one stands out more for me. Perhaps this issue is not totally unique to MCC, as it is a very common issue at all Mennonite institutions at all levels.

As it is a Mennonite Church-supported organization, MCC has been owned by Mennonites for over 97 years. For almost one hundred years, for the most part it continues to be supported by German and French ethnic Mennonites, and MCC has carried out its service mission well. I must point out that these are like-minded, good people who have been volunteering their time and providing their services. They are people with a good work ethic who are devoted to making a difference in the lives of others around the globe. Perhaps inadvertently, however, they manage to be protectors of their people and culture by closing off work opportunities to others who are not from the same ethnic and cultural background.

At MCC, I observed that if you are an ethnic Mennonite, and you are from Canada or the United States, then you are trusted and likely to get a job. The management has not made space for people of color around the table of opportunity and decision making. This is not a priority that is practiced nor talked about by people in positions of power. Some of the hiring practices at MCC mirror nepotism: it is not unusual to see relatives hiring each other, working together in the same office area and department, or even perhaps reporting to another relative. Since this model has worked for a long time, and is still working, should we leave it alone or consider it outdated and try something else that is more inclusive? This may require Canadian and American MCC workers to consider giving up unearned privilege and collective power.

It's important to look at how Americans and Canadians can work in their own country, or in each other's country, as leaders and, worse yet, be the majority of that country's representatives and country directors in other countries around the world. In other words, as natives of these two countries, they are privileged and always eligible to take positions wherever they wish to go. People from outside of the US and Canada, however, are discouraged or not trusted or appointed to serve as country representatives in their native countries. This policy or understanding between the two countries (U.S and Canada) discriminates against other qualified people, even if they hold American or Canadian citizenship as long as they are nationals of other countries. When I asked why this I the case, a colleague told me that this is one unwritten rule that MCC practices, and he added it is time to look into it.

If it hasn't already, such a dangerous conflict of interest may create unfairness and corruption in the system. Those in positions of power to monitor policy will need to look at staff practices that intentionally result in MCC positions for personal gain or for the gain of family members, friends or business associates. As an ethnic Mennonite speaker at the Mennonite World Conference put it, "Privilege, power and wealth are dangerous to the global north." I pray and hope that MCC as an organization practices its statement of compassion and love to all in the name of Christ, and I hope that this statement comes to include everybody in terms of work opportunities, instead of excluding those who are not from the ethnic Mennonite culture.

Major Family Event: Noah's Birth

On Tuesday, August 14, 2012, our second grandchild, Noah Kaleab Abebe, was born in Pittsburgh, PA. Barbara and I made the trip to see the newborn, and he was a big boy. Of course, we had a good time with Hannah as well.

Hannah knows who we are because of our efforts to talk with her every week via Skype, and because of our visits to her a couple of times every year. However, this time we observed that she was much more comfortable with her other set of grandparents.

Kaleab is impressively involved with raising his children, and we are glad to see that.

Part V: Concluding Comments

Traveling the World

The past 40 some years has been an incredible journey. What is ironic about all of this is that my beginning did not prepare me to travel the world. Yes, I did travel around the world, and it was fun and a privilege. This was never part of my plan when I first came to America. As far as traveling was concerned, my initial plan was to simply come to America and then return to Ethiopia. I would have been happy if those simple travel plans had worked out. None of what happened concerning my travel to different countries was not in my original master plan. I was so fortunate to have had the chance to travel. Although most of my travel was work-related, I was one of those people who looked for opportunities to get involved even when it required more investment in time and funds. When I was working in higher education, some travels required applying for grants and competing with other applicants, as was the case with the Fulbright. I initiated a good number of these travels and fulfilled all the necessary requirements in order to qualify for any grant award.

I was fortunate to have had the opportunity to travel to the following countries: Canada, Cambodia, Thailand, Kenya, Tanzania, Zimbabwe, Botswana, South Africa, England, Germany, France, Brussels, Italy, Holland, Poland, the (former) Soviet Union, the Czech Republic, Belize, Mexico, the Dominican Republic, Guatemala and Colombia. Within the United States, I have been to 34 of the lower 49 states, and of course, I have lived in five states: California, Indiana, Kansas, Illinois and Wisconsin.

America and Me

America is known as the land of opportunity. I have lived in the United States more than I've lived in my birth place of Ethiopia. I feel that I am just as connected to this country as anyone born and raised here. Ethiopia raised me and shaped me with good culture and traditions that I cherish. They are special and I call them mine. When I came here, my new country picked up where Ethiopia left off and provided me with all kinds of opportunities.

This is a country I came to with the intention to improve my life, and it helped me do just that. This is a country that gave me all the opportunities to help me shape my life. America made it possible for me to earn the highest academic degree possible, a Ph.D.

I had a good profession and I made a good living to support my family, both here and in Ethiopia. Despite the impediments along the way, such as the racism and classism in America, and having to deal with the white supremacy that people of color face on a daily basis, I still think this is a country where one can make it if committed to working hard and making an honest living. Of course, you also have to stay out of trouble.

I still think America is the most highly sought after country. People all over the world desire to come here. Most people who want to come here simply don't understand the real challenges they will face upon arrival. Coming to America could indeed be a wonderful opportunity for most. Its doors are open for anyone, and initially it's a welcoming nation.

Of course, as good as the American political and social systems are, America continues to have problems just like anywhere else. America does not have a perfect system by any means and needs improvement. There are many social and political problems. Sometimes it seems like anyone can be deceptive and abuse the system, doing harm until they are caught. This is especially true for those who can afford to hire a good attorney, which provides a person with a very real chance of surviving a criminal charge.

However, sometimes the crime is so bad and obvious that no attorney can save the corrupt. On the other hand, it seems as if the system provides opportunities for corruption in politics and business. The past several years alone, a couple of state governors (one in Virginia, more than two in Illinois and also a number of lawmakers to name a few) were tried, convicted and sentenced to serve time in prison.

I am also impressed by the American culture of volunteerism, which promotes helping others in need. Of course, as we all know, volunteerism is found in affluent societies, but still, people are generous and want to help others. Where I come from, people also help others in need, but not so much on an organized basis. In Ethiopia, it can happen in the spur of the moment. Most retired people in the States would like to volunteer simply so that they can stay busy by doing good for others.

Young and Still Growing

Compared to where I come from, America is a young country (239 years old), and it is still a nation in the making. America is still defining itself by categorizing people by color, nationality, and class. The Civil Rights movement helped shape the country in a major way. As it has been said, America is a nation of immigrants. People are still coming from other countries in the hopes of making it here. Immigrants from all over the world have come here, and the cultures, arts, and sciences they brought with them continue to shape the country.

Even today, America's immigration system is still in the making. It is not working as well as it should be. In the past 5-10 years alone, the country has tried to figure out what to do with Hispanic and Mexican immigrants. An estimated 12 million of these immigrants are here illegally. The issue of racism, and whites' fear of losing power, has intensified over the past several years.

The issue has been politicized; even trying to define who is an "American" continues to be an ongoing problem. Specifically, African Americans are still having a hard time because of racism. In 2014-2015 alone, there were race-related killings in Ferguson, MS, New York, Baltimore, Ohio, and now in Charleston, NC. In this last incident, a white member of a hate group killed nine black people in a church after he prayed with them.

This nation, which was originally composed of Native Americans some 400 years ago, is still trying to classify and define itself as a country of white people. The rest of us are considered aliens by some.

The country is divided by cultural and social issues. Unfortunately, this is a country mainly led by those with money and power. Since money is power, those in power use their money to influence people; they use television and other mediums to convince them of what to do and believe.

I am amazed by so many people around the country who are easily influenced by money and small talk. There are some who believe whatever these politicians tell them. They simply believe without asking any questions about outcomes or accountability.

What All This Meant?

In case you're wondering what this is all about, please read on. I am well aware that every person has their own experiences and their own stories to tell. I know that no two people who are unrelated have the same life journey. Speaking about my own journey, I can say there is no one that I know who is as fortunate as I am. I have lived a complex and profound life that is second to none. I was blessed with family, good finances, a good profession, and travel opportunities.

My journey is not only about all of the good things I have experienced, but the growth I've experienced as well. I've benefited from the challenges in my life. I enjoyed the great things in this journey of mine, but I also had a good share of social problems that I had to deal with day in and day out. However, this is not to say that I was more burdened with problems. It's simply to say that I had my fair share, and that in many ways, I learned from each encounter. As a person, I've grown enormously from it.

My professional experience is nothing short of a miracle. The friends I gained through my journey were phenomenal. Some, whom I met in college, became lifelong family friends. Through the years, sometimes by luck and sometimes by design, our family always had enough. We were comfortable financially. We are relatively well-educated and enjoying the American middle class life experience. I always say to myself, what more can I ask for?

It gives me pleasure to see where my family is now. As a family, we all are now taxpaying, responsible citizens making a major impact in communities in which we live. Some of us go to church, we volunteer, and we serve, or have served, on not-for-profit local boards. Most of all, we have become socially conscious, peace loving, and compassionate individuals who are interested in peace and justice for all.

For now, as I am 66 years old and contemplating retirement, my plan is to critically think about retirement and what it means, including coming up with a plan for how to finance my retirement years and how to even look for something to do after a formal retirement.

At this point, I am not sure that I know what living in retirement means to me and my family. For sure, I pray for good health and meaningful free time. I have no known hobbies or special skills to keep me busy. If and when I can afford it, I have plans to travel to Ethiopia every other year to visit my homeland and my family. Whenever possible, I would like to spend time with my grandchildren.

The 2015 Abebe Reunion

The first ever Abebe family reunion in the United States! This is a very significant and special event. How it came about is also very interesting. About a year ago, Surafel's family visited us in Indianapolis. During a conversation, one of his daughters (Lydia Assefa), who was only 12 years old at the time, raised a very good question. As we were all mesmerized by her level of thinking, we wanted to know what her questions and concerns were. She said, "We need to have a family reunion." She went on to say that she had not seen all of my Abebe relatives, and certainly did not know them all well. She said, "We need to hear stories from the oldest family members about why you all came to the States, and what motivated you to do what you did. We also need to know how to relate to all of our relatives. We need to know why the original four members came to the States, and how you helped others to follow you."

As a result, Lydia and Barbara were charged with the task of coming up with a plan. This is how the Abebe family reunion was born. Lydia and her mother Jessica did a wonderful job planning and communicating with the rest of us for a year. The coffee ceremony they planned gave it a special touch. As a member of the planning committee, Barbara did an outstanding job pulling all the loose ends together and organizing the event around Ethiopian colors. She also designed special t-shirts for all of the participants. What Barbara came up with was a real surprise to everyone, even to me.

Since our family reunion was historic and special, I invited my son Kaleab to write reflections on the event. The following are Kaleab's remarks:

"Growing up as a first-generation Ethiopian-American, my perspective on the "closeness" of family was different than most other kids my age. Many families in the Midwest tend to stay in close proximity to their extended relatives, sometimes with adult children living several houses down from their parents. I noticed this with my wife's family, and while this is purely anecdotal, I wondered if this close proximity made holidays, family reunions, and other special occasions less "special".

"On the other hand, the Abebe family was on the opposite end of the spectrum. From Colorado, to Michigan, to Indiana, to Minnesota, and to Ethiopia, the Abebe's were literally spread out across the country. As a result, major holidays such as Thanksgiving and Christmas were big deals. I remember being ecstatic about jumping in the car to drive to Big Rapids, MI or Indianapolis, IN to see all of my aunts, uncles, and cousins. And upon arriving at our destination, my brother and I would spend the holidays playing and eating, knowing we may not see our cousins for several months.

"*Fast forward 15-20 years. The parents, aunts, and uncles are aging and heading toward senility. The children and cousins are careening towards middle age and some have children of their own. So, it was with great anticipation that I drove to Amigo Center, in Michigan for the first family reunion with my family in tow. Not only was I excited to re-connect with family members who I hadn't seen in a while, but I was thrilled to meet new family members. The family dinner on Saturday as well as the nightly campfire sessions provided a venue for adults and children to tell stories about growing up in Ethiopia as well as the United States.*

But perhaps the most fulfilling part of the family reunion was observing my children, Hannah & Noah, throughout the weekend. It's a surreal experience to watch your own children enjoy things that you yourself remember experiencing as a child: playing soccer with cousins, eating injera and wat, and enjoying s'mores by the campfire. I can only hope that as we continue these reunions, they have the same level of excitement to see their grandparents, aunts, uncles, and cousins as I did when I was their age."

My Final Comments

I am finding it difficult to stop writing. My mind is beginning to open up its faucet wide and pour out many important, memorable moments that I forgot. As I read and re-read what I have recorded, I am delighted by what is coming back to me. I am also reaching the point where I am actually asking myself what is and is not important to write. It would have been nice to hear my children or grandchildren direct me in what to tell them. For now, I am going to pause for a while and think over what I have done.

The takeaway from this exercise is that I had the willingness to take the risk of starting my writing. This was coupled with the idea of probing my own mind and trying to remember what is certainly fading away from my memory.

Once I started outlining what I wanted to do, I actually found it to be a pleasant experience to remember all of my childhood memories. Writing about struggles during adolescence and remembering the responsibility that comes with growing up as a young adult was the thrill. At the same time, I was reminded growing up most us did not get a free ride in life.

I also learned that when writing this kind of personal document, there was no way to keep on writing without going back to look at what I'd written a couple of days ago. Many times I found it necessary to go back and fill in the blanks on a segment I had written about a specific topic, which I previously thought was very much complete and yet I discover again needed some more work.

Keeping busy with my work did also make it challenging for me to find the time to concentrate and write about my journey. I was traveling a lot and just couldn't find time to reflect on my personal life. As my wife kept reminding me, it had to stop at some point. I reached a time when that point had come and I had to find a good editor to read and organize my work. When I started writing a couple of years ago, I did not think that I would write this much. However, once I started writing, my mind was ready to supply me with more and more topics to write about. My struggle has been sorting through everything; deciding what's most important has been my biggest dilemma.

Sometimes I learned about the incompleteness of a segment of the story after I shared the story with one of my brothers. Hearing from my brothers helped me to recall more things, which made my stories much more complete. On the other hand, recalling more events meant writing more. I was torn by what to include and what to leave out, and of course, I had to decide what would be useful to my readers.

I hope all of my family members, including siblings, children, and grandchildren, as they get older, will find this short personal story to be inspirational. Perhaps it will inspire them to tell their own stories. This story is mine, and yet it is very connected to all my family. I am grateful that I'm able to share it with everyone.

To my brothers:

Yes, we come from the same background, but we traveled different roads. Each of us has had different life experiences. As a family, we all have done well. Those of us who came to the United States, we had one goal in mind: a college education, and that is just what we did. The original four (which I call the first generation), we share 11 university degrees, of which three are Ph.Ds. The second generation of our family is not far behind, earning nine university degrees, including one JD, one

MFA and multiple Ph.Ds. As brothers, we've even gone beyond our own expectations.

You have worked hard, you have been up and down, and most of all, in order to succeed, as the saying goes "you have pulled yourself up by your bootstraps." You all have good and powerful stories to share, and I believe each of your stories is as important as mine and should be available to your family to read.

To our children and all other relatives who were born in the United States:

Your experience is totally different from those of us who came from Ethiopia. Your challenge will be very different from ours, because the time you are living in is totally different, and so are the politics and social issues. You will have many choices and opportunities, so do not be afraid to take risks. Your education will be more expensive than your parents. You will have more opportunities to go into more focused and specialized skills gained through college education, which will help you stand out from the crowd. I encourage you to aim high and get the best education you can. You will be challenged by many things in life, and I hope my story will motivate you to never be discouraged.

I encourage you to always remember that you are endowed with unique gifts, talents and capacities that will enable you to change the world. Remember, it starts with you and it is your opportunity.

It is important for you to know that you are exceptionally lucky to have come from a tradition, history and legacy second to none. Always know yourself and claim your roots, and be aware of who you are (your identity) in the midst of confusion. Think outside of yourself and do all that you can to make a difference in someone's life. Believe me, it will give you happiness.

All of your relatives, I mean *all* members of your family, from near and far away places, rich and poor, educated and uneducated, are important persons in your life, because they are part of you. Just as organisms such as algae and fungus depend on other living organisms to survive, you, too, can't make it alone. The rule of common good over individualism dictates that you must share what you have with others and ask for help when you need it. As you're all well aware, this is not unique to our family, and yet, some of our family members have "made it" and now live a comfortable life. Others, on the other hand, are more in need than those of us who are more fortunate with where we are in life. However, we must believe that all of us can bring something to the table. Perhaps, instead of money or an educated mind, some of us will bring wisdom and life experience, which are equally important to building community. I heard someone say, "family first, money second, and then things." Always try to be the best you can be in everything you do, and document your journey for the next generation.

Conclusion

Here are some concluding thoughts. I want my readers to know that this is not a comprehensive story of my life or my families. This is a small slice of a reflection on my journey. There are many delightful, hilarious and remarkable growing-up-day stories that are not included in this memoir. Some of these stories could easily be lost in translation, and in the process, they simply lose their impact

I can say I lived a simple and yet solid life. I worked hard, learned a lot, enjoyed my past and I now anticipate the future. I was blessed by love of family and friends. I made a respectable and honest living; helped others when I was able to; and I openly shared those stories. I was enriched by my experience, and I think I am a better person because of it. This journey has been worthy, and I would do it all over again.

In the process of writing this book I came to recognize that my journey was meant to be confronted frequently by many challenges. These challenges, for the most part, were nothing more than to serve me as speed bumps to help me reflect, think, and assess where I am heading. I now realize that they were not intended to keep me from going forward.

I have come a long way, and I plan to continue my expedition forward on the same pathway with the understanding that there are limitations that come with age and that there will be many unknowns in front of me.

I hope you enjoyed reading my story. Now my hope is to live long enough to experience more of my sons' and grandchildrens' voyage. As I anticipate retirement, I plan to devote more time to stay in touch with relatives in the U.S. and in Ethiopia. Now I leave you with one of my favorite scriptures:

Jeremiah 29:11-13

11 For I know the plans I have for you," declares the Lord, "plans to prosper you and not to harm you, plans to give you hope and a future. 12 Then you will call on me and come and pray to me, and I will listen to you. 13 You will seek me and find me when you seek me with all your heart."

Glossary

1. Afework Tekle...One of Ethiopia's most celebrated artists, known in particular for his paintings on African and Christian themes as well as for his stained glass

2. Alemitu...A land owner

3. Asegedech...My sister-in-law

4. Ashenafi...My youngest son

5. Awassa...A resort city in the south of Ethiopia

6. Baher Dar...A city in northern Ethiopia

7. Dembi Dolo...A city in western Ethiopia

8. Deder...The Ethiopian town where I was born

9. Derege...A good friend from high school

10. Derg...The Ethiopian political party of the 70s

11. Dire Dawa...The largest city in the Harar Province

12. Gashe Mehari Indale...One of my good friends in Addis

13. Gedamu...My older brother

14. Haile Gebrselassie ...A world famous long distance runner

15. Harar Province...A state

16. HMMMH – A training hospital in Nazareth, Ethiopia

17. Iteye Aregash...One of my very good friends in Addis

18. Kaleab...My oldest son

19. Kelemua...My niece

20. Kulube...An Ethiopian town

21. Ledet...One of my nieces

22. Merkato...An open market

23. Mismake...My younger sister

24. Nazareth...The Ethiopian city where I went to high school

25. Sisay...My brother next to Mismake

26. Soka...A small Ethiopian village where I lived

27. Solomon...My brother next to Teshome

28. Tadelech...My older sister

29. Tamene...The youngest of my siblings

30. Teshome...My younger brother

Publications

Book Review:

Abebe, Z. (1999) Beyond our prayers [a review of the Lancaster Mennonite Conference answered God's call to serve in Ethiopia and the birth of Meserete Kirsitos Church (MKC) of Ethiopia]. *The Mennonite Quarterly Review.*

Book Chapter:

Abebe, Z. & Claassen, R. Co-authored a chapter in the upcoming book to be published *"Restorative Justice in Unusual Place"* by Criminal Justice Press NY. 2010.

Articles:

Abebe, Z. (November 2015) Hope for the Future; *The Mennonite*

Abebe, Z. & Claassen, R. (Spring 2007) Higher Ground – Conflict Resolution in Colleges and Universities. *Restorative Discipline.* The Association for Conflict Resolution Magazine (pp. 12.15)

Abebe, Z. (January 2007). *The Tragedy of Racism: The Two Faces of Racism – Underserved Discrimination and Undeserved Privileges.* Submitted as a chapter for a book to be published.

Abebe, Z. (April 2006). *Unique Discipline Process empowers Students to Resolve Conflict.* Student Affairs Today (9) 1, 3.

Abebe, Z. & Abebe T. (2004) Curriculum Transformation to Prepare Students for a Diverse World. Direction: A Mennonite Brethren Forum 44(2) 195-200.

Abebe, Z. (2002). Speaking of People (Abebe on Multicultural Education) Addis Tribune, March 1, 2002 Addis Ababa, Ethiopia. An article published in Addis Tribune while leading the Goshen College Study Abroad program.www.addistribune.com/archives/2002/03/01-02/Dr.htm

Abebe, Z. (2001).Moving forward using the skills of all members. *The Mennonite* 4(9),15.

Abebe, Z. (1998) Focusing on the future by looking at the past. *Black Issues in Higher Education*, 14 (24), 76.

Abebe, Z. (Eds.). (1996). Moving Beyond Awareness: A Model for Multicultural Education and Curriculum Infusion, Goshen, IN. (*Published with support from Lilly Endowment Grant from Indianapolis and distributed to 410 members of Council of Independent Colleges.*)

"Affirmative Action: Necessity or Obstacle." The Goshen College Record.

"Multicultural Education in the Year 2000." *Black Issues in Higher Education,* 8(16), 10.

"The Contributions of Foreign Scholars and Issues Related to Their employment." *A Bi-annual Journal of International Education,* 19(1), 26-36.

Courses Taught

- Introduction to Psychology
- Life Span
- Mind Power – to selected early adolescence students
- Adolescence Psychology
- Analysis of Racism and Power
- Conversational Amharic Course for Study Abroad to Ethiopia (Goshen College)

Printed in the United States
By Bookmasters